JESUS POLITICS

How to Win Back the
Soul of America

Phil Robertson

NELSON
BOOKS

An Imprint of Thomas Nelson

Jesus Politics

© 2020 by Phil Robertson

Published in Nashville, Tennessee, by Nelson Books, an imprint of Thomas Nelson. Nelson Books and Thomas Nelson are registered trademarks of HarperCollins Christian Publishing, Inc.

Published in association with Yates & Yates, www.yates2.com.

Thomas Nelson titles may be purchased in bulk for educational, business, fundraising, or sales promotional use. For information, please e-mail SpecialMarkets@ ThomasNelson.com.

ISBN 978-1-4002-1018-3 (audiobook)
ISBN 978-1-4002-1007-7 (eBook)
ISBN 978-1-4002-1006-0 (HC)
ISBN 978-1-4002-2555-2 (custom)
ISBN 978-1-4002-1019-0 (TP)

Library of Congress Control Number: 2020936457

Printed in the United States of America

23 24 25 26 27 LBC 9 8 7 6 5

CONTENTS

Introduction   vii

PART I: JESUS POLITICS IN THE VOTING BOOTH

Chapter 1.   A Kingdom Manifesto   3
Chapter 2.   The Kingdom Foundation   13
Chapter 3.   On the King's Capital   27
Chapter 4.   On Gun Ownership in the Kingdom of Love   43
Chapter 5.   On Biblical Environmentalism   55
Chapter 6.   On Life According to the King   73
Chapter 7.   For the American Family   87
Chapter 8.   For Kingdom-Centered Healthcare   103
Chapter 9.   Of Mercy and Forgiveness   115

PART II: SHARING JESUS POLITICS IN EVERYDAY LIFE

Chapter 10. The Law and Order of the King   131
Chapter 11. Changing America Through Kingdom Living   143
Chapter 12. Taking the Manifesto to the Street   157

Jesus Politics: The Kingdom Manifesto in Action   173
Notes   175
About the Author   181

INTRODUCTION

On a November morning in 1976, my son Al and I were driving up Highway 165 toward Ouachita Christian High School. From the river basin, we made our way north, past the cotton fields of north Monroe, past the moss-covered cypress trees of Bayou Desiard, past the prehistoric banks of Black Bayou. Radio on, some DJ in middle Monroe played our favorites: Lynyrd Skynyrd, the Allman Brothers, ZZ Top. And as we pulled into the school parking lot, he interrupted one of our favorites, the Charlie Daniels Band classic "The South's Gonna Do It Again," to announce that Jimmy Carter, the governor from Georgia, had beaten Republican incumbent Gerald R. Ford. Carter would be the next president of the United States.

Truth be told, I wasn't all that politically aware. I knew Uncle Sam had led the troops to war in Vietnam, a war in which our country's armed forces had managed to snatch defeat from the jaws of victory. I knew that in the wake of the war, President Richard Nixon had resigned after authorizing the break-in at the Watergate hotel, the headquarters of the Democratic National

Committee. I was vaguely aware that a group of Middle Eastern kings had turned on an oil shortage in 1973 and that oil shortage was driving up gas prices. The country was disenfranchised. I knew that much. And maybe a southern boy from Georgia could turn it around.

"Things are looking up, Al," I said. "The old southerner made it through."

"Maybe so, Dad." Al said.

And that was the extent of our political conversation about the presidential election of 1976. In fact, that'd be the only political conversation I'd have with anyone until sometime in 1978.

I was a new Christian in those days, just a year or so removed from my lawless living (and just a few years since being an outright fugitive, a story I shared in *The Theft of America's Soul*). I'd been saved by the glorious gospel of our Lord Jesus Christ, raised from the waters of baptism and into a new life in Jesus. I was living a life of obedience, one committed to prayer, and studying God's Word. I'd been teaching at Ouachita Christian High School and had transformed into a productive member of society. But busy as I was amending my lawless ways, I hadn't spent an ounce of energy on politics.

Politics wasn't a topic we discussed much growing up. In fact, I only recall one political conversation in my childhood. My father had fallen off a drilling rig while on the job in south Louisiana, and he'd busted himself up pretty good. There'd been some discussion about whether he should apply for government assistance, but Dad shot the idea down as soon as it'd taken flight.

"Nah," he said, "we'll manage without the government," and we did.

The community rallied around our dirt-poor family. Church members brought us food. Our neighbors helped us tend to the chores around the house while Dad regained his strength. The months passed, and we managed to make it through none the worse. Dad made it back to the rig, and though he never said it, I received the message loud and clear: river rats needed a government safety net as much as we needed a hole in our hoop nets.

Months passed after the election of 1976, and still I was politically unmotivated. But as I continued to walk into my new life, an odd thing happened. My spiritual epiphany led to a political awakening. And it all started with the Word of God.

ALL THE SCRIPTURES POINT TO A KING

As I studied the Bible, I began to notice something curious. From Genesis to Revelation, I saw a theme threading through. It was a political theme, though it wasn't a democratic one. Time and time again, the Scriptures spoke of God the Almighty, the King of kings and Lord of lords. He was the sovereign ruler, and he made no bones about it.

I noticed the kingly thread in Exodus. There, Moses led the Israelites away from the tyrant king of Egypt and toward the promised land. As they marched from Egypt and toward the land God would give them, they worshipped and sang, "The LORD reigns for ever and ever" (15:18). On that long journey to the promised land, the Almighty called to Moses from a mountaintop. There, he told Moses he was establishing "a kingdom of priests and a holy nation" (19:6). Who reigned over that kingdom? The Lord, the one who was leading them home. Only one chapter later, the Almighty laid down the law of that kingdom, giving Moses the Ten Commandments.

In Deuteronomy, the sovereign theme appeared again. There, Moses reminded the people of the laws handed down from the mountain. He called the people to live by those laws of God, the God whom Moses called the "God of gods and Lord of lords, the great God, mighty and awesome, who shows no partiality and accepts no bribes" (10:17). *Lord.* What is that if not a term of kingship?

In Daniel, an earthly king fell on his face and recognized that his sovereignty was no match for that of the Almighty. The evil ruler Nebuchadnezzar of Babylon, the king who'd persecuted God's chosen people, fell before the Almighty's prophet and declared, "Surely your God is the God of gods and the Lord of kings" (2:47). Nebuchadnezzar, the most powerful king of his age, recognized that there was an authority greater than his own.

I flipped to Psalms and found still more kingly references. The psalmist wrote, "The LORD has established his throne in heaven, and his kingdom rules over all" (103:19). He'd been the king forever, the one who ruled over the wandering Israelites, over Nebuchadnezzar, and over my little plot of land on the Ouachita River.

I discovered that the prophets spoke of the King, too, and they recognized the King demands holiness. Consider Isaiah. After his vision of the Almighty, he cried out, "I am ruined! For I am a man of unclean lips, and I live among a people of unclean lips, and my eyes have seen the King, the LORD Almighty" (6:5). In his presence, Isaiah confessed just how unholy he was. In the presence of the King, Isaiah repented.

The sovereign thread ran through the Old Testament, but it

didn't stop there. It carried through into the New Testament, the testament of the King who came from heaven to earth.

In the gospel of Matthew, John the Baptist stood preaching in the wilderness, preparing the people for the coming of the Christ and warning, "Repent, for the kingdom of heaven has come near" (3:2). Just one chapter later, Jesus came on the scene, and he offered a slight variation on the message, one I might paraphrase this way: "John said the kingdom of God was near, but take a look at me; the kingdom of God is here, because the King is here!" (4:17).

Throughout his ministry, Jesus didn't mince words about his kingship. When Jesus met Nathanael, when he told the would-be disciple where he'd been just the hour before, Nathanael declared, "You are the king of Israel" (John 1:49). I reckon Jesus could have corrected the confession. He didn't.

In the gospel of Luke, the Pharisees asked Jesus when God's kingdom would come. Jesus gave it to them straight: "The kingdom of God is in your midst" (17:21).

In the gospel of Matthew, Jesus sent his disciples into the countryside. He gave them simple instructions:

Do not go among the Gentiles or enter any town of the Samaritans. Go rather to the lost sheep of Israel. As you go, proclaim this message: "The kingdom of heaven has come near." Heal the sick, raise the dead, cleanse those who have leprosy, drive out demons. Freely you have received; freely give. (10:5–8)

Who'd given them these instructions? The one who'd brought the kingdom with him. King Jesus himself.

In the gospel of Mark, Jesus made some bold claims. He shared about his coming suffering and death. He taught, "Whoever wants to be my disciple must deny themselves and take up their cross and follow me" (8:34). But then he offered his followers the most astounding promise: "Truly I tell you, some who are standing here will not taste death before they see that the kingdom of God has come with power" (9:1). See his words? The kingdom would come with power before the disciples died. Why? Because he, the King, had come to bring the kingdom. It was a bold statement, one that locked down the time line. The kingdom was already on earth, right in their midst.

Even in Jesus' last hours, Pontius Pilate asked him a pointed question: "'Are you the king of the Jews?' Jesus answered, 'You have said so.'" (Mark 15:2). These were the last words Jesus said before being handed over to the guards. And what did the guards do?

> They put a purple robe on him, then twisted together a crown of thorns and set it on him. And they began to call out to him, "Hail, king of the Jews!" Again and again they struck him on the head with a staff and spit on him. Falling on their knees, they paid homage to him. And when they had mocked him, they took off the purple robe and put his own clothes on him. Then they led him out to crucify him. (vv. 17–20)

The guards were clueless. They didn't know they were murdering the King of the universe. Still, Mark recorded their words as an affirmation of the truth. Even a tortured Jesus was recognizable as the King.

After Jesus' death, resurrection, and ascension, his people

continued to follow King Jesus, continued to carry his message into the world. During Paul's ministry, he visited the Gentile churches, "preaching the kingdom" (Acts 20:25). While under Roman guard, Paul held a round-the-clock revival, "explaining about the kingdom of God" to the Jews living in Rome (Acts 28:23). He stayed under house arrest in Rome for two years, and while he was there, "he proclaimed the kingdom of God and taught about the Lord Jesus Christ—with all boldness and without hindrance" (Acts 28:31). He wrote letters to his protégé, the young Timothy, in which he offered these closing lines: "Now to the King eternal, immortal, invisible, the only God, be honor and glory for ever and ever. Amen" (1 Tim. 1:17).

To put an exclamation point on it all, the Spirit of God visited the apostle John while he was exiled on the island of Patmos for his belief in King Jesus. During that visitation, John was given a vision of King Jesus, one he described in this way:

I saw heaven standing open and there before me was a white horse, whose rider is called Faithful and True. With justice he judges and wages war. His eyes are like blazing fire, and on his head are many crowns. He has a name written on him that no one knows but he himself. He is dressed in a robe dipped in blood, and his name is the Word of God. The armies of heaven were following him, riding on white horses and dressed in fine linen, white and clean. Coming out of his mouth is a sharp sword with which to strike down the nations. "He will rule them with an iron scepter." He treads the winepress of the fury of the wrath of God Almighty. On his robe and on his thigh he has this name written: KING OF KINGS AND LORD OF LORDS. (Rev. 19:11–16)

THE KING'S OPPOSITION

As I studied the Bible, I found another truth too. There's opposition to the reign of King Jesus, a false kingdom controlled by the evil one. Paul put it this way: "For our struggle is not against flesh and blood, but against the rulers, against the authorities, against the powers of this dark world and against the spiritual forces of evil in the heavenly realms" (Eph. 6:12). It couldn't have been plainer. The evil one had his own political system, his own false kingdom, and it stood in opposition to the rule and reign of King Jesus. Those powers influenced so many in the world around us, people who lived as enemies of the cross. What would their end be? As Paul wrote, "Their destiny is destruction" (Phil. 3:19).

I began to understand there was a spiritual war between two competing kingdoms: the true kingdom of King Jesus and the false kingdom of the evil one. And that war was playing out in the world around me, influencing my friends, my family, my community, and my country's politics. As a follower of the true King, shouldn't I do whatever it took to bring the kingdom of God to earth as it is in heaven? Shouldn't I do my best to bring love, life, peace, and spiritual prosperity to a world of chaos and death?

I continued learning about the competing kingdoms, and as I did, I shared with anyone who'd listen. I shared it with my old running buddies, folks like Big Al Bolen, the redneck teacher from Arkansas who'd become an atheist under the influence of his university professors. I shared it with men and women who were down and out, who'd grown so dependent on government assistance that they refused to work. I shared it with women who'd had abortions and the men who'd paid for them. I shared and shared and shared. As I did, I realized just how much the war between the kingdom of heaven and the false kingdom of the evil one was playing out in everyday politics in America.

- Through the political process the government had removed God from the public schools and given people like Big Al atheism in its place.
- Through the political process the government had legalized abortion in 1973, sanctioning the murder of millions and saddling the men and women who sought them with guilt and shame.
- Through politics America had been given a welfare system that locked its people in hopeless poverty.
- Through politics the government had liberalized sexuality, removing it from the confines of marriage.
- Through politics America had begun to call lawful what the Bible called lawlessness.

The more I paid attention, the more I saw it. The evil one—the power of this dark world—was pushing his agenda down on the American people through the democratic process. The result? We were becoming more ruthless, more brutal, and more lawless. A nation of death headed for destruction.

It all came to a head on a sweltering evening in 1978. Miss Kay and I stood on the banks of the Ouachita River and discussed my political awakening. I hadn't put it all together, but it seemed to me the war between good and evil was being fought in Washington. The battle for America's soul was being waged in the political arena. And if that were true—and I was convinced it was—it was time to understand some things, time to figure out who I was politically.

"Could you find me a rundown of the political platforms, Miss Kay?"

"You can't be serious, Phil," she responded, knowing how little I'd cared for politics just months before.

"Serious as a shotgun," I said. "As a member of the kingdom of God, I need to see which side lines up more closely with the principles of the King."

WHERE IS THE KING IN MODERN AMERICAN POLITICS?

These days, it's mighty hard to find the King in our political parties, and that goes for both Republicans and Democrats. Our news cycle is dominated by partisan bickering. Both sides spin up millions of dollars through campaign contributions and gin up as much dirt as they can on the opposition. Both sides claim only they can sort out the problems that plague our country. It's a cycle that continues election after election. But look around. Are things getting any better?

We're more divided than ever. We're so divided, in fact, that we choose our news outlets based on whether we're right-wingers or left-wingers.

We're more violent than ever, a country that routinely experiences mass shootings at the hands of demonically influenced lunatics.

We're more immoral than ever, a country entertained by programming that contains illicit sex. (Which is to say nothing of the filth on the internet.)

The family is in decline.

Babies are being aborted.

There are riots in the streets.

What was once called evil is now called good.

And if all of this isn't bad enough, so many of our politicians, the folks who are supposed to be "for the people," fall prey to corruption. Though they're supposed to represent the people, they make a fortune from the business of politics.

What's the problem?

Listen up, America.

There's a vast difference between the Supreme Court and the Supreme Being. The King's laws for living supersede the laws of any man-made rules and regulations. What's more, the King's laws have eternity riding on them. But the sad truth is, though we were once a country who did their best to follow the King, we've traded God's laws for laws fashioned in the shape of our own desires. "We the People" have cast our votes for the politics of self-indulgence, self-interest, and self-gratification. We've voted for the very things that steal our freedoms, kill our society, and destroy our country. And we did all these things without checking in with King Jesus first.

Yes, in our delusion, we've decided we're capable of governing ourselves without reference to the policies of King Jesus, policies established in love. And man-made laws based on our finite judgment have only ever led us astray. There's good news, though. As followers of Christ, we've been given the antidote to America's soul sickness. What's the antidote? Jesus Politics.

Jesus—God with Us—came in the midst of an ancient political quagmire. He made his home with the Jewish people, a people who were under the left thumb of godless political rulers (the Romans) and the right thumb of God-forgetting religious leaders. In that broken political system, he announced the truth. He was the King, and aligning ourselves with his ways would lead to peace, prosperity, and a full life, even in the middle of so much brokenness. That's not all, though. Jesus also tasked us to pray that his kingdom would come on earth as it is in heaven. And in addition to praying, he asked us to bring the kingdom into the world around us through every means possible, including, if possible, political means.

In this book, we'll explore the problems facing America and the King's policies as to each of those problems. I'll offer the King's declarations about those problems and the declarations that make up his Kingdom Manifesto. Then I'll share how you can use your vote to advance the Kingdom Manifesto.

AMERICAN POLITICS ARE NOT JESUS POLITICS

In 1978, Miss Kay brought me a stack of papers on the policy positions of Democrats and Republicans. I studied them and tried my best to determine which party might advance the policies of the King, promote the policies of the King, and protect the policies of the King. I knew there were good Democrats, of course, men like President Carter who proclaimed himself born-again and taught Sunday school. But as I examined his party, I noticed how so many pushed hard against the Scriptures, how they relied on the government more than God. They wanted the King out of the public schools, and they wanted to replace him with an atheistic philosophy. They promoted the liberalization of sex and treated the orgasm as the pinnacle of the human experience. The doors to abortion on demand had been opened by the Supreme Court, and many Democrats vowed to protect the right of a mother to terminate her child. Sure, some were more conservative on the issues of morality and sexuality, but for the most part, they were described well by the Scriptures as "God-haters, insolent, arrogant and boastful; they invent ways of doing evil" (Rom. 1:30).

Then there were the conservatives, folks who believed in smaller government and personal responsibility. They weren't interested in taxing me to death, though I was dirt-poor at the time and didn't have anything besides beans and appaloosa catfish to tax. Republicans seemed to promote religious liberty and moral living, and a great number of them pledged allegiance to King Jesus. They hoped to overturn legalized abortion. They held to biblical standards for what constitutes a family. The conservatives wanted America to remain rooted in the ideals this country was founded on, namely, ideals of faith, freedom, and family. To be fair, they weren't perfect. Many didn't have a great track record of caring for the poor. More than a few were greedy or immoral in their own right. Some were a little too cozy with lobbyists and special-interest groups. But as I began to understand the direction of their party, I was convinced.

After reading through the party platforms and stewing on them for a few days, I told Miss Kay, "Well, I guess I'm a Republican." She nodded. She'd read those platforms and made up her mind days before.

"I guess I am too, Phil," she said.

In the years that followed, I did my best to understand the goings-on in American politics. I kept up with the party platforms and weighed them against the principles of the kingdom. Best as I could, I voted in alignment with those principles. And truth be told, I never thought my opinions about politics would count for much in the public square. I figured I'd live my life as a quiet river rat, scratching out a cornbread living as a duck call salesman, and doing my best to influence the direction of American politics from the grass roots. I didn't expect I'd be on a television show that'd become a worldwide phenomenon. I didn't know people would give a rip about my thoughts on politics. But as a result of our family's success through *Duck Dynasty*, the unthinkable became a reality. The King gave me a platform to share about his kingdom. As a result, I've spoken at certain political events, such as the Conservative Political Action Conference, and stumped for some Republican candidates. Each time I speak, I make it clear: I'm more interested in advancing policies that align with the kingdom of heaven than I am in advancing the agenda of any political party.

So no matter what side of the political aisle you choose, know this: *if you are a member of the kingdom, King Jesus makes demands on your life.* This includes the political candidates you support, the political groups you give your money to, and the votes you cast. So as for me and my house, we:

- Donate to prolife and pro–religious liberty policy groups
- Cast our votes for those who side with and advance the politics of the King
- Share the good news of the King with the people in our lives in the hope they might become members of the kingdom and might use their voices and votes for King Jesus

Will you join me in advancing the policies of King Jesus? In order to do it, we'll have to know and understand King Jesus' positions on the issues of the day. Do you know them?

In this book, I'll share what I've learned in seven decades of kingdom living. I'll share how we can turn from the politics of self-indulgence, self-interest, and self-gratification—namely, the politics that have dominated our democracy for the majority of my lifetime. We'll see how the followers of King Jesus have the antidote for the political ills of our country. And what's that antidote? *Jesus Politics*.

So come with me as we look at the problems facing America and explore how we might address them as members of the kingdom. Explore a new way of thinking and acting, a way that follows the declarations of the King. Adopt Jesus Politics as your manifesto. If enough of us do, maybe we can turn this country around. Maybe we can live to see a country that once again proclaims "In the King we trust."

PART I

JESUS POLITICS IN THE VOTING BOOTH

CHAPTER 1
A Kingdom Manifesto

It was not a typical morning on the river. I'd rolled out of bed early, just like any other Louisiana morning. I'd brewed a pot of coffee, black as tar. But this morning I wasn't heading out to the shop or down to the fields. I wouldn't be walking through the cypress groves or picking mayhaws on the banks of the Ouachita. I wasn't headed anywhere but to my La-Z-Boy, in fact, because the river had spilled out of its banks and flooded most of God's country.

In late April the storm clouds typically come and stay awhile, soaking northern Louisiana in their annual floods. But that day the driveway in front of the house was underwater. The river had risen into Miss Kay's pavilion less than twenty yards from the backdoor. I was all hemmed in.

I switched the news on and Joe Biden filled the screen. He had a message for America, he said, but before he got to it, he replayed the 2017 footage of some white supremacists carrying torches and spewing hate in Charlottesville, Virginia. He shared President Trump's comment after the attacks, in which the president said there were "very fine people on both sides" (a comment I don't believe the president was ascribing to tiki-torch-carrying white supremacists). Mr. Biden said that President Trump posed a threat to this country and that the American people were locked in a "battle for the soul of the nation." What's more, he implied that he was the solution to the perceived problem, and if America didn't vote for him, America would fall apart.

It is true. The white supremacists carrying the torches around Charlottesville in August 2017 were sinners slinging demonic hate and vitriol. It is also true that America was locked in a battle for its very soul. But what wasn't true was that Donald Trump had created the problem or that a long-serving politician could somehow be the solution to it.

Liberals, that is, the ones who promote the slaughter of their children while saving the whales, they're the fix for America's problems?

The folks who legalize all sorts of sexual immorality and perversion, they're the ones with the moral authority to govern this country?

The people who spew as much profanity and filth as anyone, they're the alternative to hateful speech in our country?

The party who booted God out of the public schools, they're the ones who can save us?

Hey, Mr. Biden, your hypocrisy is showing!

There's no doubt we're locked in a battle for America's soul. And Mr. Biden, if you're reading along, pay attention. The problem with our country isn't a problem that can be solved by any particular political party. After all, America's problem isn't a flesh-and-blood problem; it's a powers-and-principalities problem.

As I wrote in *The Theft of America's Soul*, the evil one is working overtime to convince America that God is dead or, at the least, God is unnecessary. The evil one's convinced us that our freedoms weren't founded in God, but rather they were granted to allow us to chase our every desire. The evil one twisted those desires and used them to influence the way we vote. As a result, the Enemy has sneaked into America through politicians who reflect the character of its people. And what is that character? The apostle Paul put it this way:

> For although they knew God, they neither glorified him as God nor gave thanks to him, but their thinking became futile and their foolish hearts were darkened. Although they claimed to be wise, they became fools and exchanged the glory of the immortal God for images made to look like a mortal human being and birds and animals and reptiles.
>
> Therefore God gave them over in the sinful desires of their hearts to sexual impurity for the degrading of their bodies with one another. They exchanged the truth about God for a lie and worshiped and served created things rather than the Creator—who is forever praised. (Rom. 1:21–25)

What are the characteristics of those who follow the evil one? They are a people who don't worship God. A people whose hearts are foolish and darkened. A people who worship the animals, the environment, maybe even the climate. A people who are sexually immoral, who serve every lust. Sound familiar?

Yes, Mr. Biden, we're certainly locked in a battle for the soul of America. If we're going to win that battle, though, we need a spiritual solution, not one born from the hearts of men. And as people of the King, as citizens of the kingdom of heaven, we need a strategy for bringing that spiritual solution "on earth as it is in heaven." We need a common strategy, a statement of purpose. What do we need? We need a kingdom manifesto.

THE POWER OF A MANIFESTO

In 1848, Karl Marx and Friedrich Engels wrote a pamphlet that changed the world—but not for the good. That pamphlet served as the basis for their now-famous work *The Communist Manifesto*, which led to the rise of godless red states such as the USSR, the People's Republic of China, and Cuba. It was a document meant to highlight the problems with capitalism and Western democracy, and it argued that those forces oppressed disadvantaged people by controlling property, production, and the political elite. It made a case for a socialist revolution and claimed that when the people rose up, when they redistributed wealth, land, and education, a great utopia would arise. But who would oversee the redistribution? The writers of the manifesto and their followers, of course.

The great communist utopia would follow. *How'd that work out for you, Russia?*

It was a manifesto bound to fail from the beginning because there was no God in it, no room for the Almighty to work through it. It was a political philosophy that led the people to place their faith in government, but a government made up of wicked men.

Marx himself was no Christian, and when his manifesto was adopted by Vladimir Lenin, it became an even more atheistic document. In fact, quoting Marx, Lenin wrote, "Religion is the opium of the people—this dictum by Marx is the cornerstone of the whole Marxist outlook on religion. Marxism has always regarded all modern religions and churches, and each and every religious organisation, as instruments of bourgeois [the materialistic ruling class] reaction that serve to defend exploitation and to befuddle the working class."[1]

Befuddle is a word that should have been applied to their political ideology but was instead applied to the things of God. See how twisted their thinking is?

The Communist Manifesto was a provocative document. It didn't mince words and it called for action. And I guess you could say it was successful in moving people toward a certain philosophy, even if that philosophy was foolish and bankrupt. Even today we still have socialist and communist countries, including China, North Korea, and Cuba. Even today we have politicians like Vermont senator Bernie Sanders and New York representative Alexandria Ocasio-Cortez who promote communist ideals under the moniker of democratic socialism.

Old Marx's manifesto has fooled the fools. I wonder if he's laughing in his grave.

Karl Marx and his commie buddies corrupted the word *manifesto*. But what if we reclaimed and redeemed the word? After all, a manifesto is no more than a declaration of intent, whether for good or bad. It's a decisive, provocative statement of action. Manifestos typically aren't politically correct. They don't coddle those who disagree. And manifestos aren't just for the communists. Maybe we Christians, the citizens of the kingdom of heaven on earth, need our own manifesto. Maybe we need a unifying call to action for all citizens of the kingdom of heaven on earth.

DO WE REALLY NEED A MANIFESTO?

I trust old Noah Webster, an early American educator who understood the power behind a just form of government. In his 1834 book *Value of the Bible and Excellence of the Christian Religion*, he wrote:

> The command of God is, "He that ruleth over men must be just, ruling in the fear of God," 2 Sam. 23:3. This command prescribes the only effectual remedy for public evils. It is an absurd and impious sentiment, that religious character is not necessary for public officers. . . . But in representative governments, if rulers are bad men, it is generally the fault of the people.[2]

Webster was an educator at heart and a godly man, and he did his best to promote and preserve a tradition of biblical governance. He knew that America's success was dependent on the people electing just, wise leaders. He also knew the religious character of a country is derived from the religious character of the people. If old man Webster could look at our country today, don't you think he'd agree that we need a manifesto?

Webster created the first American dictionary, a dictionary that did not shy away from religious or political terms. In that dictionary, he defined the term *manifesto* as "a public declaration, usually of a prince or sovereign, showing his intentions, or proclaiming his opinions and motives; as a manifesto declaring the purpose of a prince to begin war, and explaining his motives."[3] A strong definition, wouldn't you say?

But considering Webster's definition, maybe you're wondering, *What gives you the right to create a manifesto, Phil? You're no prince.* Maybe that's true in the earthly sense, but consider the spiritual truth laid out in the Scriptures. The apostle Peter calls me a member of the royal priesthood, a man called to "proclaim the excellencies of him who called you out of darkness and into his marvelous light" (1 Peter 2:9 ESV). In other words, the Bible itself includes us in the royal line, and it gives us the authority to proclaim, declare, and promote the will of King Jesus. As part of the royal line, we're to pronounce the truth of the King, warn of his coming judgment, and help create an environment conducive to the spread of the kingdom of heaven on earth.

As a member of the royal family of King Jesus, I'm advancing his purposes by offering a clear declaration of intent for voting Christians. It's a sort of new political manifesto for the citizens of the kingdom of heaven on earth, and it addresses how we ought to assert our heavenly citizenship through the democratic process. But before we get started, you need to know this: I didn't get the terms of this manifesto from the Republican National Committee or the National Rifle Association or any conservative political action committee. I didn't get them from Laura Ingraham or Sean Hannity at Fox News. (The truth is, I reckon they see me as something of a strange duck.) Nor did I crib the ideas of this manifesto from the platform of any political candidate. No, the positions contained in this Kingdom Manifesto were not provided by any human. Instead, these are the talking points I believe that come straight from the Almighty, derived from his Bible. These are the answers I've come to after forty years of studying God's Word.

A DECLARATION OF INTENT
FOR CHRISTIANS

In this book, we'll dig into the pressing issues in the current American political landscape. We'll address those issues by answering three simple questions in each chapter:

- What's the problem?
- What's the King's answer to the problem?
- How do we put the Kingdom Manifesto into action?

In the final chapter, we'll collect each of the statements of intent, each of the declarations into a final Kingdom Manifesto, a manifesto that embodies the politics of King Jesus. We'll use that manifesto as a statement to guide our votes and ensure that we promote those who protect and advance the principles of King Jesus. And if there's no perfect candidate on your ballot, no godly man or woman running for a particular office, we'll identify the candidate who lines up the closest with the Kingdom Manifesto and cast our vote accordingly.

It's true, we are in the thick of a war for America's soul. It's a real war with serious consequences. This book is a call to all citizens of the kingdom of heaven on earth to wake up spiritually and politically and join in the battles of that war. It's a call to come together and move with intent. After all, this country won't make it another generation unless a mighty throng of Christians uses their democratic freedoms to advance the policies of King Jesus. Are you ready to join that throng as part of the kingdom of heaven on earth? Are you ready to learn what Jesus Politics is all about and use your vote in a way worthy of the King? Come on. Let's join together in creating a Kingdom Manifesto.

CHAPTER 2

The Kingdom Foundation

Every spring the rains come heavy on the Ouachita River. Come March, the storm clouds roll across the southwest, dumping hundreds of thousands of gallons of water across eastern Texas, southern Arkansas, and northeast Louisiana. That water collects in basins, flows into creeks and streams, and feeds into the Ouachita, which flows southward just below my home. All that water creates a yearly flood cycle, one we've become accustomed to. Still, there are years when the waters creep a little too high even for the most veteran redneck river rats. And even for me.

In 1991, the Robertson homestead was pretty sparse. We were living hand to mouth, still pouring all our money into a business that was just starting to take off. Miss Kay and I were raising our boys in a rickety old home, something that might look like one of today's cheaper modular homes. Our homeplace was thrown together with the materials we had at hand, and to say it wasn't the most structurally sound dwelling might constitute the biggest understatement in this book. Still, we had a roof over our head. We had a sufficient number of beds. There was a furnace. And truth be told, we got along just fine even though we were living well below the poverty line.

Our home had been built on the banks of the river, in the floodplain. The far end had been built on stilts. During some particularly wet seasons, the water rose all the way to those stilts and settled just below the floorboards. They'd never risen high enough to infiltrate the house (it'd take a flood of biblical proportions for that to happen) or compromised the structural integrity of the house. Then again, the water had never risen as high as it did in 1991.

From April through May of that year, our region of the country received something near twenty inches of rain. Day and night, week after week, it was one continuous rainstorm. As it filled the Ouachita basin, worry set in. The water came up, rising up the stilts of our home and settling under the house, less than a foot from the floor. And that's where it stayed for almost a month.

Now you might not be particularly up to speed on the ins and outs of residential construction. At the time, I wasn't particularly savvy as to the ways in which excess moisture affects flooring materials. But it doesn't take a rocket scientist to understand what happens when warm, stagnant water just sits for a month under a home with exposed plywood flooring. Allow me to share my firsthand experience.

When river water is just a few feet from the underside of your house, the humidity rises and presses up against the underside of that plywood. The plywood wicks up the humidity and holds it in its pores. After a while, moisture-laden plywood loses its structural integrity and becomes something akin to soaked cardboard.

And then, even if the water recedes, the floor remains compromised. Even weeks after the water recedes. How do I know?

Early in the morning hours, well before the sun rose over the river, I woke to something that sounded like the house settling just a bit. Then I heard the creaking of shifting flooring. Then something buckled and there was a thunderous cracking sound. Jarred out of bed, I ran into the living room. There, where the couch used to be, was a gaping hole. And as I walked to that hole and looked down, I was greeted by the eyes of Old Blue, my Catahoula Cur, who slept under the house. Neither of us made a sound.

Of course, we replaced the floor. Of course, I used sturdier material the second time around. Of course, we made sure there was a sufficient moisture barrier under the house so we'd never lose another couch and our Catahoula Cur wouldn't be in danger again. But since that night in 1991, the night a kind of sinkhole appeared in my living room, I've come to two conclusions.

First: Don't let your Catahoula sleep under a rotting house.

Second (and more important): If you don't build your house with the right materials, the floor will fall out from under you.

THE FOUNDATION OF AMERICA: JESUS POLITICS

I've done the work. I've read the research. I've studied how the Founding Fathers built our country, and I know the materials they used for its foundation. And no matter what any revisionist historian says, no matter how hard they try to convince you otherwise, know this: the United States of America was built on a godly foundation, a kingdom foundation.

In October 1829, Noah Webster wrote a letter to James
Madison that recounted their history together, how they met in
1782, when Webster visited Philadelphia (the seat of the young
US government at the time) to share the early drafts of a small
book. That book eventually grew into a two-volume dictionary,
the one we all know and love today. But Webster wasn't writing
to discuss his dictionary. So once he'd dispensed with the pleas-
antries, he launched into his thoughts on a far more important
matter: the drafting of a new constitution for the Commonwealth
of Virginia.

In his letter, Webster offered his well-reasoned opinion about
the role of the Almighty in government:

> I sincerely hope that Virginia, in her new Constitution, will
> avow some fundamental errors, in the principle of representa-
> tion, which, in my opinion, have marred the constitutions of
> other States, & may yet shorten the duration of our republican
> form of government. I know not whether I am singular in the
> opinion; but it is my decided opinion, that the christian reli-
> gion, in its purity, is the basis or rather the source of all genuine
> freedom in government. I speak not of the religion which gives
> the property & power of a state to [maritus] & dignitaries.
> I speak of the religion which was preached by Christ & his
> apostles, which breathes love to God & love to man. And I am
> persuaded that no civil government of a republican form can
> exist & be durable, in which the principles of that religion have
> not a controlling influence.[1]

Webster was a man of opinion and conviction. And it was his
opinion and conviction that Virginia—and by extension, all of

America—needed an unshakable, immovable, bedrock foundation. That foundation was Christianity.

Webster wasn't alone, of course. As I wrote in *The Theft of America's Soul*, many (if not all) of the Founding Fathers considered the Bible as the foundation and framing of our country. And though I'll not retread all that ground here, I'll recap a little. Consider George Washington, a devout Christian, who knew virtue and morality couldn't exist without the influence of God. In his 1796 farewell address, Washington said, "Whatever may be conceded to the influence of refined education on minds of peculiar structure—reason & experience both forbid us to expect that National morality can prevail in exclusion of religious principle."[2] He added, "To the distinguished Character of Patriot, it should be our highest Glory to add the more distinguished Character of Christian."[3]

John Adams, the second president of the United States, affirmed that same foundation:

> The general principles, on which the Fathers achieved independence, were the only Principles in which that beautiful Assembly of young Gentlemen could Unite. . . . And what were these general Principles? I answer, the general Principles of Christianity, in which all these Sects were United.[4]

In fact, Adams also believed a system of laws based on God's Word would lead to a virtuous utopia, a veritable paradise.[5]

Patrick Henry, a devout Christian, stated, "The great pillars of all government and of social life . . . [are] virtue, morality, and religion. This is the armor, my friend, and this alone, that renders us invincible."[6]

James McHenry, a signer of the Constitution, believed the Bible should be protected, preserved, and distributed and that it should form the basis upon which our society is built. He wrote:

> Public utility pleads most forcibly for the general distribution of the Holy Scriptures. The doctrine they preach, the obligations they impose, the punishment they threaten, the rewards they promise, the stamp and image of divinity they bear, which produces a conviction of their truths, can alone secure to society, order and peace, and to our courts of justice and constitutions of government, purity, stability and usefulness. In vain, without the Bible, we increase penal laws and draw intrenchments around our institutions. Bibles are strong intrenchments. Where they abound, men cannot pursue wicked courses.[7]

The Founding Fathers knew the Scriptures, and they would have understood the teachings of Jesus in the gospel of Matthew. In the Sermon on the Mount, he preached about good deeds, hate, adultery, and divorce. He taught us to love our enemies and to give to the needy. He taught us to pray, fast, and store up treasures in the hereafter. And as he concluded his sermon, he ended with a simple teaching:

> Therefore, everyone who hears these words of mine and puts them into practice is like a wise man who built his house on the rock. The rain came down, the streams rose, and the winds blew and beat against that house; yet it did not fall, because it had its foundation on the rock. But everyone who hears these words of mine and does not put them into practice is like a foolish man who built his house on sand. The rain came down, the

streams rose, and the winds blew and beat against that house, and it fell with a great crash. (Matt. 7:24–28)

It's safe to assume the godly men who founded our great republic knew the trouble that comes when a country is built on the flimsy philosophies of men. After all, they'd experienced firsthand the issues that came with a self-serving, man-centered, truth-denying, tyrannical monarchy. They'd suffered under British tyranny, a tyranny imposed by a man-appointed, godless king. So they came together under the belief that a biblical foundation would create something different. Something just and peaceful and loving. Something kingdom centered. Something as enduring as the Scriptures themselves. After all, to paraphrase the Scriptures: "All governments are like grass, and their glory is like the flowers of the field; the grass withers and the flowers fall, but the word of the Lord endures forever" (1 Peter 1:24–25).

THE PROBLEM: REVISIONIST HISTORY AND JESUS-LESS POLITICS

We've entered a new era in American history. Once, we were a country founded on Christian principles. We were a people planted on God's Word. Then our Christian principles came under attack as a government of godless men sought to kill God, as they removed the statues, signs, and symbols of our country's biblical heritage from the public square. That wasn't enough, though. Now, our very right to express our personal faith in schools, politics, and even our own businesses is under attack. Our right to operate charitable foundations based on our biblical worldview is too.

Consider, for example, how our politicians have disregarded the Founding Fathers' wisdom and wishes. Consider how they've done their level best in recent decades to remove God from our public schools. In the early 1960s, the Supreme Court ruled that teachers and principals couldn't lead prayers, but they didn't stop there. Christian symbols were systematically removed from schools too. Even today those symbols continue to be removed. In fact, during the writing of this book, a group that calls itself the Freedom From Religion Foundation requested that an Ohio middle school remove a plaque of the Ten Commandments hanging at the school. This, despite the fact that the plaque was a gift to the district from the graduating class of 1926 and that it had been on display for nearly a century without objection.[8]

Likewise, politicians, courts, and citizens alike have targeted Christian symbols on public land, some of which have stood for decades without objection. For instance, the Supreme Court declared that certain state courthouses cannot publicly display the Ten Commandments, even though a depiction of Moses carrying the commandments is displayed on the frieze of the Supreme Court building. As I noted in *The Theft of America's Soul*, ordering the removal of the Almighty's legal code from local courthouses is odd, because a violation of nearly any of those commandments will land you in legal hot water.

If the removal of God from public schools and government buildings isn't bad enough, state governments are cracking down on the private exercise of religious beliefs too. In 2012, Jack Phillips, a Colorado baker, refused to bake a cake for a same-sex couple. Why? He's a Christian man, someone who believes that biblical marriage is between a man and a woman. What's more, he had the audacity to allow his Christian beliefs to influence his business practices. And it bears mentioning that he founded, owned, and operated that private business. Imagine that.

What was the result of Phillips standing by his convictions? The couple filed a complaint with the Colorado Civil Rights Commission and claimed that Phillips had broken a state law by denying "the full and equal enjoyment of the goods [or] services . . . because of . . . sexual orientation." The same-sex couple prevailed and, as reported by the *Los Angeles Times*, "Colorado has barred Phillips from making any more wedding cakes because he refuses to abide by its civil rights laws."[9]

A private baker, who runs a private business, cannot exercise his religion through that business? (Say what, Colorado?)

I suppose it's fair to say that Colorado's antidiscrimination legislation allowed certain kinds of discrimination. Evidently, discrimination against Christian faith passes the smell test.

Still, there's a bit of good news. Phillips appealed the decision of the Colorado courts, and the case made its way to the hallowed halls of the Supreme Court of the United States. There, a group of black-robed legal scholars found that the Colorado Civil Rights Commission had violated Phillips's constitutional rights and reversed the commission's decision because they'd shown "clear and impermissible hostility" toward his religious views.

But don't let the good news warm your heart too much. Months after the decision, Phillips was again sued because he refused to bake a cake celebrating a Colorado resident's gender reassignment.

And the hits keep coming.

It's not just Colorado bakers who've come under fire for acting on their religious views. Consider the news out of Philadelphia, the former national capital where godly men first framed our Constitution. There, the city took action against Catholic Social Services (CSS) because, "as a Catholic agency, CSS cannot provide written endorsements [for foster parenting] for same-sex couples which contradict its religious teachings on marriage." This, despite reporting that "not a single same-sex couple approached CSS about becoming a foster parent between its opening in 1917 and the start of the case in 2018."[10] There were, of course, many other fostering agencies who'd approve same-sex couples. Still, the city of Philadelphia, in its grand wisdom, decided that shutting CSS down because of their religious beliefs was a viable option, even though the city had an urgent need for foster families.

Doesn't that sound like brotherly love?

THE CHRISTIAN RESPONSE: RETURN TO OUR FOUNDATION

Up until the American Revolution, liberty—particularly religious liberty—was an ideal at best. But our Founding Fathers knew true and lasting liberty could only be established when the people of this country recognized that all were created equal and that they were endowed by the Almighty with certain inalienable rights. (For those of you not so fluent in eighteenth-century English, *inalienable* means "can't be taken away.") The foundational right, the one embodied in the First Amendment, was the right to practice one's Christian faith.

Didn't the Founding Fathers know best?

We are living in an age when the new state religion is atheism and governments are removing expressions of faith left and right. We're living in an age where government actors are trying to shut down the practice of our faith in the public square, where an increasing tyranny of godlessness seeks to silence us. Are you okay with this? I'm not.

American Christian: *It's time to bow up, to take some responsibility.*

The organizers of the American Revolution were godly men who took Jesus' message in Matthew 7:24–27 to heart. They wanted nothing more than for *you* to have the freedom to practice your Christian beliefs. They wanted you to exercise your faith in both your public and private life. They wanted you to speak out about it and to assemble together in your church. More than anything, they wanted you to build your life and the life of this country on the only sure foundation: the foundation of King Jesus' Word.

MANIFESTO IN ACTION

If Jesus were to come down from on high to speak directly to our country's politics today, I believe he'd urge us to speak out and act on our faith. He'd encourage us to

- Elect politicians who refuse to pass ordinances and laws requiring citizens of the kingdom to compromise on their values
- Elect godly men and women who will pass laws that protect our religious liberties, our freedom to call sin what it is, and our freedom to invite your neighbors into the kingdom of God

- Elect those who will vet all judges and confirm only those who honor and uphold the godly heritage of our country
- Elect judges who will uphold the constitutional rights of the people and strike down any laws that infringe on our religious liberties
- Empower those who are morally upright, who demonstrate allegiance to King Jesus in the way they speak, act, and treat others

I can see the question turning over in your mind, especially as it relates to the last item.

What if no godly men or women are running, Phil? What if neither politician in any given race is morally upright?

In that case, I suppose we ought to vote for those politicians who'll protect our rights to express our faith, regardless of their own behavior. Men and women who might be works in progress from a biblical perspective, but who wouldn't enact laws or confirm judges who'd shut down the citizens of the King.

So as you go into the voting booth, in the next election cycle or any other, ask yourself these questions:

- Which candidate will protect my right to express my religious beliefs in the public square?
- Which candidate will protect my right to express my religious beliefs in my private business?
- Which candidate will appoint judges who understand the importance of religious liberty, who will help us return to the sure foundation of God's Word?

- Which candidate will stand up to the atheists who would build a country on a plywood foundation?

And once you've come to a godly conclusion, do your duty. Act on the King's manifesto and do your part to rebuild the foundation of America on godly principles.

A KINGDOM MANIFESTO

THE PROBLEM:
American politicians are undermining the
godly foundations of this country by promoting
a godless, atheist agenda that is eroding the
religious liberty of the citizens of the kingdom.

THE MANIFESTO OF THE KING:
We must rebuild the foundation of this country,
returning to the Word of God and protecting the
religious liberty of the citizens of the kingdom.

A MANIFESTO IN ACTION:
Vote for leaders who will promote religious liberty,
protect our rights to practice Christianity in every
public square, and live lives aligned with Jesus Politics.

CHAPTER 3

On the King's Capital

I support the Red.

Ain't that a loaded comment?

Now, when I say the Red, I don't mean the red flags of socialism. I'm not a card-carrying communist. I'm not a fan of the former USSR, whose government headquarters was Red Square in Moscow.

I'm not a Red China sympathizer either.

And if it's not clear already, I certainly don't support the modern red sympathizers in American politics, such as Bernie Sanders or Alexandria Ocasio-Cortez, who call themselves democratic socialists. (What is a democratic socialist anyway?)

And, no, I'm not referring to red states either, that block of states that mostly vote for Republican candidates.

No, when I say I support the Red, I mean I support old Jimmy Red, the redneck up the road.

These days, I count Jimmy Red as a good-enough fella. He's a hard worker. Tough as nails. But this wasn't always the case.

For years, old Red was on the welfare roll. Why? Raised poor, with little opportunity, not a whole lot of education, and little access to money, it was difficult for him to find long-term work. He took jobs from time to time. Construction. Fishing. Hauling. But nothing ever stuck. So he used the government to fill the gaps.

I knew Jimmy, though, and I'd been neighbors with him for years. I knew, with a little opportunity, a little access to resources, he'd work hard and do just fine. So I hatched a plan. I bought a truck, one that Red could use.

Months after I bought that truck, I stood on an old rutted road near my homeplace. A film crew had come to talk about my thoughts on welfare. Instead of just sitting in my recliner and discussing the problems with socialized government programs, I decided to take them on a little field trip. I wanted them to see what happens when one redneck offers another redneck a leg up. I wanted to show them how to eliminate the welfare state in America.

We made our way to a place where Jimmy Red was in his truck, hard at work under the afternoon sun. He was busy smoothing out the potholes created by heavy traffic during a particularly wet season. As his truck pulled around a blind corner, I shared the story with the film crew. How I'd bought that old eighteen-wheel hauling rig that Jimmy used to move stone, gravel, dirt, whatever. I held the title to the truck, but I'd told Red, if he'd get his commercial driver's license, he could use the truck for construction jobs and keep whatever he made off the hauls. He had to pay for his own gas and insurance, of course. And any permitting too. But I promised Jimmy I wouldn't take a red cent of his profit, and I kept my word. To date, I haven't made a dime off of his hauling business.

When Jimmy turned off the rig and stepped out of the cab, I called him over to the patch of road where I was with the film crew. In a camouflage LSU hat and sleeveless T-shirt, he smiled for the camera.

"You're a redneck, let's face it," I said.

"No doubt," he said.

"I'm an educated redneck, almost on the line to where some say, 'He ain't a redneck no more.' But redneck roots go deep, don't they, Red?"

Red nodded and laughed.

I shared how Red had become a hard worker, the type of man who'd become quite industrious since he jumped off the welfare roll. He moved dirt, hauled stone, did a little excavation work, I said. But that wasn't all. With the money he made from his hauls, he'd begun reclaiming junk for resale, stuff his wife called *antiques*. He bought it for pennies and sold it for dollars. Jimmy Red, I said, had become an entrepreneur. A certifiable capitalist.

I pointed to the patch of ground Red had smoothed over, showed how it'd been leveled so it was passable.

Jimmy looked down and kicked at the dirt, but I knew he was proud of his work. He'd done something of value, and he'd earned a day's wage as a result.

After the interview, I went back to the house, and I thought about old Red. He was a man without any prospects a few years ago. Someone who didn't have a job or a means to provide food, outside of fishing (and maybe some occasional poaching). He'd once been comfortable taking the taxpayers' money, but now, he'd been given an opportunity to earn his wages through hard work. He'd more than made good on it. And how had he gotten that opportunity? Through Robertson-care, my personal program to end local poverty, which comes with only one condition: use what you've been given to earn a living.

Old Jimmy Red has been hauling for me for some time now. And though he's not rich in an earthly sense, he makes enough money to get along. He has plenty to eat, his family has what they need, and he's not dependent on the government to get ahead. Why? Because one redneck used his capital to help out another redneck.

But Robertson-care isn't just about providing earthly opportunities. Just as I offered Red an earthly opportunity, I've also held out heavenly opportunities too. Just as I've shared my capital, I've also shared the good news of the Almighty. Why? Because capitalism isn't just about creating economic opportunity for those around you. It's about paving the way for the saving message of Jesus.

THE PROBLEM: WHO DECIDES HOW TO SPEND YOUR MONEY?

Socialism is a man-made economic ideology driven by the big idea that the masses know how to use *my* property, *my* money, and *my* materials better than I do.

It's the ideology that gave birth to government-run housing, welfare, socialized medicine, and a tax system that redistributes the wealth of hardworking Americans to non-working Americans. And I suppose if we lived in a kingdom-centered society, a world in which *We the People* followed the directives of the King, I might be more inclined to go along with such a notion. But our society is controlled by a different kingdom, the kingdom that leads the people according to their desires instead of according to what's godly. Yes, the kingdom of the evil one has established itself in America, and what's the result? The apostle Paul might put it this way:

> For, as I have often told you before and now tell you again even with tears, many live as enemies of the cross of Christ. Their destiny is destruction, their god is their stomach, and their glory is in their shame. Their mind is set on earthly things. (Phil. 3:18–19)

Does that sound like a group of people you want directing your tax dollars, your property, and your economic opportunities?

No way, dude!

Generally, it's worth noting that much of the government's spending is wasteful. For instance, while writing this book, I discovered the government paid millions in licensing fees for green camouflage meant to be used in the Afghani *desert*.[1] As the head Duck Commander, I know a thing or two about camouflage, and I can tell you for certain that anyone wearing lush green in a land that is primarily desert might as well have a target painted on their back.

While I could give hundreds of examples of wasteful government spending—spending as wasteful as producing camo that doesn't match the environment—that's not my primary concern. Instead, I'm concerned that when a government composed of ungodly bureaucrats exercises control over our wealth, they'll spend it on ungodly policies. I'm concerned that in their well-meaning attempts to create government programs, they'll end up using our money to fund immorality. Don't believe me?

Pay attention, Mr. and Mrs. and Ms. Taxpayer.

In 2010, President Barack Obama signed a bill making socialized healthcare available to the masses through government intervention. Sure, the government system is slow, full of bureaucracy, and too expensive (just like all socialist programs). That alone would be enough to criticize it. But as is the way with all government intervention, Obamacare, as it's come to be known, is also a vehicle for advancing a godless, immoral agenda.

How?

In the runup to the 2020 election, a group of politicians (supporters of socialized medicine) came clean about their intentions for socialized healthcare. For years, there'd been a bill on the books (my son Al tells me it's called the Hyde Amendment) that in most instances prohibits the use of federal funds to pay for abortions. But as the 2020 electoral cycle opened, the majority of Democrat candidates shared an expanded view of a pro-choice agenda, arguing that Obamacare recipients should receive some form of abortion coverage. There was a holdout, though. Former vice president Joe Biden had previously stood by prohibiting government-funded abortions. But as he entered the race, he was criticized for his support of the Hyde Amendment. So Old Joe flipped and changed his position. The *New York Times* reported, "Joseph R. Biden Jr. . . . no longer supports a measure that bans federal funding for most abortions."[2]

Show us your true colors, Joe.

See what happens when socialist systems are directed by godless people? We end up with government-directed policies that fly in the face of the Almighty. Government-funded immorality. Government-subsidized death. And the American people are forced to hold their noses and choke it down.

THE CHRISTIAN RESPONSE: THE FREEDOM TO USE CAPITAL FOR THE KING

You might argue capitalism is its own sort of-ism, and in the hands of godless people, it can be just as destructive. True enough. But ask yourself, *Which philosophy—capitalism or socialism—gives the citizens of the kingdom the best opportunity to use their money to advance the causes of the King?* The one that allows a godless government to distribute wealth as they see fit or the system that gives kingdom people the freedom to direct their resources toward godly causes?

Do I really need to ask?

The King could have come and set up a holy socialist government that redistributed wealth to the poor. But if you examine the Scriptures, you'll see that's not what happened. Instead, the King entrusted his people with money and asked them to use it in ways that honored the King.

Throughout the Bible, the Almighty affirms private wealth creation. In the book of Proverbs, Solomon wrote, "Lazy hands make for poverty, but diligent hands bring wealth" (10:4).

In the book of Deuteronomy, Moses handed down the economic policy statement of the Almighty (among other policy statements and laws, of course). Throughout the book, the Almighty seemed to affirm the private ownership of wealth, and he directed his people to use it freely to help others. Consider his version of privatized welfare:

> If anyone is poor among your fellow Israelites in any of the
> towns of the land the LORD your God is giving you, do not

be hardhearted or tightfisted toward them. Rather, be open-handed and freely lend them whatever they need. . . . Give generously to them and do so without a grudging heart; then because of this the LORD your God will bless you in all your work and in everything you put your hand to. There will always be poor people in the land. Therefore I command you to be openhanded toward your fellow Israelites who are poor and needy in your land. (15:7–8, 10–11)

In the same way, God's people are meant to use their resources to employ those in need. Again, in Deuteronomy, Moses shared the Almighty's fair-wage policy:

Do not take advantage of a hired worker who is poor and needy, whether that worker is a fellow Israelite or a foreigner residing in one of your towns. Pay them their wages each day before sunset, because they are poor and are counting on it. (24:14–15)

The theme of using personal wealth to care for the poor continues throughout the Scriptures. Solomon wrote,

- "Whoever oppresses the poor shows contempt for their Maker, but whoever is kind to the needy honors God" (Prov. 14:31).
- "Whoever is kind to the poor lends to the LORD, and he will reward them for what they have done" (Prov. 19:17).
- "The generous will themselves be blessed, for they share their food with the poor" (Prov. 22:9).
- "Those who give to the poor will lack nothing, but

those who close their eyes to them receive many curses" (Prov. 28:27).

Likewise, Jesus taught his disciples about money and how they should use their hard-earned wages to invest in the economy of the kingdom. He said, "Sell your possessions and give to the poor. Provide purses for yourselves that will not wear out, a treasure in heaven that will never fail, where no thief comes near, and no moth destroys. For where your treasure is, there your heart will be also" (Luke 12:33–34).

He shared how using our property, money, and material to serve others was the same as serving him, and he said that kind of kingdom spending would lead to heavenly reward:

He will put the sheep on his right and the goats on his left.

> Then the King will say to those on his right, "Come, you who are blessed by my Father; take your inheritance, the kingdom prepared for you since the creation of the world. For I was hungry and you gave me something to eat, I was thirsty and you gave me something to drink, I was a stranger and you invited me in, I needed clothes and you clothed me, I was sick and you looked after me, I was in prison and you came to visit me." (Matt. 25:33–36)

Jesus preached about how we might use our wealth for the good of others, but he also taught about the dangers of hoarding. He warned how trying to hold on to wealth can pull us away from what really matters.

In fact, when a wealthy young ruler—a young man who had stored up a considerable fortune—asked what he could do to enter the kingdom of heaven, Jesus said, "If you want to be perfect, go, sell your possessions and give to the poor" (Matt. 19:21).

The rich man, however, loved his money and couldn't do it. So he turned his back on Jesus.

What was Jesus' response? It was pretty tough: "I tell you, it is easier for a camel to go through the eye of a needle than for someone who is rich to enter the kingdom of God" (v. 24).

That wasn't all either. Jesus warned, "Life does not consist in the abundance of possessions" (Luke 12:15). He taught that the riches of the world could choke out the seed of faith (Mark 4:19). He said we should serve the King above our business interests because "no one can serve two masters" (Luke 16:13).

All told, Jesus seemed to speak about wealth and how to use it almost more than anything else, and the early church followed his teachings. In fact, it was the free use of their capital that helped establish and advance the early church. But don't take my word for it. Consider the Scriptures yourself. The book of Acts describes the activities of the young church this way:

> They devoted themselves to the apostles' teaching and to fellowship, to the breaking of bread and to prayer. Everyone was filled with awe at the many wonders and signs performed by the apostles. All the believers were together and had every-thing in common. They sold property and possessions to give to anyone who had need. (Acts 2:42–45)

Only a few chapters later, we learn, "There was not a needy person among them, for as many as were owners of lands or houses sold them and brought the proceeds of what was sold" (Acts 4:34 ESV). Later, Paul reminded the Ephesians:

I have not coveted anyone's silver or gold or clothing. You your-selves know that these hands of mine have supplied my own needs and the needs of my companions. In everything I did, I showed you that by this kind of hard work we must help the weak, remembering the words the Lord Jesus himself said: "It is more blessed to give than to receive." (Acts 20:33–35)

See? The Bible, the book of the King, gives us great personal responsibility with respect to how we use our money, and this is in keeping with the very life of the King himself, who, "though he was rich, yet for your sake he became poor, so that you through his poverty might become rich" (2 Cor. 8:9).

Jesus didn't abdicate his responsibility to us, the spiritually poor, and we shouldn't abdicate ours either. And we shouldn't expect the government to do our job for us. Instead, we ought to fight for the right to use our wealth to care for those in the world around us and, ultimately, to bring them into the kingdom. This is exactly what Jesus asks of us. If we don't, if we turn that respon-sibility over to the government and let ungodly legislators and presidents determine how to spend our capital, there's no doubt our money will be used for ungodly ends. There's no doubt the wealth God gave us will be redistributed to programs controlled by the evil one.

I don't expect this message will be well received. I reckon the media might take a shot or two at my view of the King's eco-nomic policy. After all, the message of the King is foolishness to those under the influence of the evil one (1 Cor. 1:18). Don't you see how true this is? All these self-proclaimed wise men, today's politicians, don't they think they know how to spend our money better than we do? But how has that panned out, America? Have socialist programs—healthcare, government housing, welfare—made us more moral, upright, godly, and harder working? Have they eliminated poverty?

Nah.

According to census statistics, 38.1 million people still live in poverty in the United States.[3] Some research shows that as much as 10 percent of government assistance recipients have used illicit drugs in the last month.[4] So, if you ask me, I'd say all those government programs haven't cured the ills of society—socially or morally.

What could alleviate poverty more directly while increasing the moral standing of our fellow Americans? Come on down to the river and find out. See how a few kingdom capitalists—my family, for instance—fight poverty, joblessness, and homelessness. Meet folks like Jimmy Red who work hard and live right. And once you're convinced (and I know you will be), join me in the fight for the right to keep your money and to use it for the King.

THE MANIFESTO IN ACTION: THERE'S ONLY ONE KINGDOM-ISM

After being on this good earth for more than seven decades, I've learned a thing or two. Among them is this: one kingdom-minded redneck can help a down-and-out redneck better than the government ever could. After all, I'm in a much better position to identify a fellow river rat who's willing to work hard and take advantage of any opportunity to get off the welfare roll and become a productive member of society. By adopting my local redneck, by helping him or her break the cycles of poverty, I'm living out the Scriptures and able to share the good news of the Almighty with him. My capital allows me entry, gives me a way to share the only-ism that transcends all-isms, namely, baptism.

Jimmy Red took the economic opportunity I held out to him. He made good on it too. And as I checked in on his progress, as we discussed his business opportunities, I shared the good news of Jesus with him. Eventually, he took me up on the invitation to follow the King of kings, and then he followed me into the waters of the Ouachita River. There, I baptized him in the name of the Father, Son, and Holy Spirit. There, he entered the kingdom of heaven, and though he hasn't lived a perfect life since his baptism (none of us has), he's experienced a life of more peace and prosperity. All because I had the freedom to direct my capital toward the purposes of the King.

As citizens of the kingdom, we ought to fight to preserve the right to use our property, money, and material to advance the kingdom of heaven, the kingdom of love. So when you enter the voting booth this year, or any other year, ask yourself the following questions:

- Which candidates will divert my money toward ungodly socialist programs, toward things like federally funded abortions?
- Which candidate will allow me to use my money as I see fit to advance the causes of the King?
- Who will advance policies that encourage responsible spending and personal choice?
- Is there a candidate who puts his money where his mouth

is and himself donates to the poor, the addicted, and the down-and-out?

Do some digging. Understand the candidates and the positions. Know how they'll spend your money. And then say a prayer and vote accordingly.

A KINGDOM MANIFESTO

THE PROBLEM:
American politicians are advancing socialist policies that
direct the wealth of kingdom citizens to ungodly causes.

THE MANIFESTO OF THE KING:
Followers of the King must be free to use
their capital to care for the poor and needy
and to advance the message of the King.

A MANIFESTO IN ACTION:
Vote for leaders who will protect capitalism,
the system that best allows the people to direct
their money toward kingdom causes.

CHAPTER 4

On Gun Ownership in the Kingdom of Love

In May 2019 two students at a Colorado high school opened fire in yet another great American tragedy. The shooters had smuggled guns onto the campus, aiming to create carnage like so many before them. But their demonic dreams of mass murder were thwarted by a small group of high school heroes. Those students were led by Kendrick Castillo, a senior at the STEM School Highlands Ranch, who lunged at one of the shooters who was brandishing a weapon. Castillo's move gave his classmates an opportunity to escape and hide. Three other students followed him, and together they pinned down the shooter. But in the process, Castillo took a bullet. And the gunshot was fatal.

Days later, vigils were organized to celebrate Castillo's sacrifice and life. But though those gatherings could have been a time to mourn, grieve, and honor the young hero, one of those vigils—organized by the Brady Campaign to Prevent Gun Violence—took a turn. In a packed gymnasium at the Highlands Ranch school, US Senator Michael Bennet[1] and Congressman Jason Crow turned the gathering into a political rally, using the victims' death to call for stricter gun legislation.

The folks in Colorado must be training up their kids in the way they should go, because they saw right through the ruse. Recognizing the political stunt for what it was, many of the students walked out of the vigil. Some news outlets reported they chanted "This is not for us," "Political stunt," and "We are people, not a statement" as they left the gym. It was also reported that some of the students who exited the rally gathered outside the school and held an impromptu rally, chanting "Mental health! Mental health!" The students refused to speak with journalists, but their chants made it clear. They understood the source of the violence in their school: the deranged, psychotic ruminations of a demonically influenced student. What's more, they understood the power of sacrifice to save a life, and they wanted nothing more than to honor that sacrifice.

The children stood up to the politicians that day, and the politicians took note. After the vigil brouhaha, Bennet and Crow made statements that didn't quite amount to apologies. (My mother always told me to offer a straight and simple apology.) A spokesperson for Bennet said, "Last night should have been about Kendrick Castillo and the STEM School students. They are our focus and the event should have been set up to ensure their voices were fully heard." Crow, however, refused to apologize for politicizing the event, stating, "It is my job to take tough questions and offer real solutions."[2]

If you haven't noticed, we've found ourselves at a crossroads in our history. According to the Center for Homeland Defense and Security, in 2018 there were ninety-seven reported school shootings as compared with nineteen in 1970. Of those ninety-seven school shootings, there were fifty-six fatalities as opposed to seven in 1970. Violence is on the rise among our youth, and they're taking it to the schools. And, yes, something has to be done about the culture of violence that's possessed our youth. But instead of addressing the demonic cause of that violence, instead of seeking solutions to deal with the hate and anger, our politicians seem more hell-bent on using the deaths of our children for their political advantage. They're using it to push an anti–Second Amendment, patently unconstitutional, anti-gun agenda.

I have a little news for you politicians: America doesn't have a gun problem. America has a hate problem, a lack of love problem. And if we don't address this problem, we'll continue to see this rash of murder and mayhem.

WHY WERE WE GIVEN THE SECOND AMENDMENT ANYWAY?

Cards on the table: I'm a gun-toting, NRA card–carrying, Second Amendment supporter. And chances are, if you're reading this book, you already knew that. I host a podcast that's fielded sponsorship requests from companies like iTarget (a home firearm training system), TacPack (a tactical gear retailer), and My Patriot Supply (a company some might call a prepper warehouse). So I suppose some might call me biased. After all, I'm an old-timey patriot who takes self-sufficiency seriously.

Our Founding Fathers took self-sufficiency seriously too.

They knew a day might come when We the People might need to defend ourselves against a tyrannical form of government that wanted nothing more than to take away our liberties, especially our religious liberties. And even though men such as George Washington, James Madison, and John Adams surely knew violent men might use guns to murder others, they made no attempt to prohibit the people from owning guns. In fact, they made gun ownership a fundamental right by way of the Second Amendment to our Constitution, which stipulates, "A well regulated Militia, being necessary to the security of a free State, the right of the people to keep and bear arms, shall not be infringed."[3]

The Second Amendment wasn't drafted to protect our right to hunt. It wasn't simply a provision to allow us to protect our homes from intruders. It certainly wasn't drafted to protect our right to let a few rounds loose at a gun range either. It was a provision passed by the Founding Fathers who knew that firearms might be necessary one day to deter future fascists.

Don't believe me? Consider what the Founders said themselves. In a letter to Alexander Hamilton, George Washington wrote:

It may be laid down as a primary position, and the basis of our system, that every Citizen who enjoys the protection of a free Government, owes not only a proportion of his property, but even his personal services to the defence of it, and consequently that the Citizens of America (with a few legal and official exceptions) from 18 to 50 Years of Age should be borne on the Militia Rolls, provided with uniform Arms, and so far accustomed to the use of them, that the Total strength of the Country might be called forth at a Short Notice on any very interesting Emergency.[4]

Similarly, Thomas Jefferson penned the following in a letter to William Stephens Smith (the son-in-law of John Adams): "What country can preserve [its] liberties if their rulers are not warned from time to time that their people preserve the spirit of resistance? Let them take arms."[5]

The right to bear arms was a nonnegotiable for our Founding Fathers. It was so important that it was the constitutional amendment that immediately followed the First Amendment, which guaranteed free speech, freedom of religion, and freedom of assembly. And this right to bear arms was held in high esteem for more than two hundred years. Somewhere along the way, though, public sentiment toward guns shifted. And though I can't say exactly when this was, I can recall the first time I ever heard a politician proclaim the murder problem in America was a gun problem. It came in the early 1980s.

THE PROBLEM: GUN CONTROL REGULATION WON'T FIX THE HUMAN HEART

On March 30, 1981, John Hinckley Jr. attempted to assassinate President Ronald Reagan. During the attack, the president, press secretary James Brady, and two others were shot. Although a bullet lodged in Reagan's left lung, he was likely saved by a Secret Service agent who threw his body between the assassin and the president. Brady, however, was not so lucky. He was shot in the head, which left him paralyzed and permanently disabled.

After the literal smoke cleared, Brady's wife, Sarah, became an activist, arguing that guns were the problem and we needed more gun restrictions in the United States. It was the first time I recall hearing the argument that guns were the problem. But it was clear to my buddies and me, rednecks who'd grown up using firearms all our lives, that the problem was not the firearm itself. The problem was Hinckley's demonically influenced state. In fact, we later learned he believed killing the president would somehow impress the actress Jodie Foster. Still, Mrs. Brady pressed on, ultimately using the tragedy to promote the so-called Brady Bill, a law that was finally passed in the early 1990s and placed new restrictions on guns. Among those restrictions, certain people—convicted felons, addicts, illegal aliens, and those with mental health issues—were kept from obtaining firearms.

Now pay close attention to what I'm actually saying. I'm not here to debate the merits of the Brady Bill. I'm saying, before Hinckley's assassination attempt, it seemed to me that all Americans knew exactly who to blame for gun violence: the perpetrator. But in the wake of this tragedy, the narrative shifted. Almost overnight, all the talking heads, all the liberal elites, all the professors in all the universities seemed to agree: gunmakers, gun owners, and even the gun itself were to blame.

That narrative has dug in like a tick, and it's sucking the lifeblood of liberty. Politicians and media personalities ask good questions—Do people have to keep dying at the hands of gun-wielding men?—but then they spin the same tired narratives in response:

- If we had expanded restrictions, these mass shootings wouldn't happen.
- If we got rid of the AR-15s, these senseless acts of violence wouldn't happen.

- We need to round up the guns like Australia did and melt them all down.

Instead of examining the real problem—the lost soul of America—they blame an easier scapegoat: guns themselves. They demonize guns and gather at town halls and in vigils and in the streets to do the same. They create more division and conflict and fuel more hate. Instead of casting out the demons that are influencing the human heart, they focus on exorcising the guns.

MORE LOVE, LESS REGULATION

Gun-control legislation will never cure what ails America. How do I know? Because murder has been in the human heart since the beginning, well before the invention of the gun. In fact, the third human being on the planet murdered the fourth. Remember the story?

Cain worked the soil. Abel kept flocks. Both made offerings to the Lord. Two boys. Two offerings. But all offerings are not created equally, just as the Scriptures record. "The LORD looked with favor on Abel and his offering, but on Cain and his offering he did not look with favor" (Gen. 4:4–5). Now I'm no expert on biblical interpretation, and I'm not sure why the Lord didn't accept Cain's offering. Maybe he held back a portion from the Lord. Maybe he didn't offer it with gratitude. Who knows but God himself? Whatever the reason, though, Cain discovered the Almighty favored Abel's offering, and Cain did not take the news well. The Bible records that Cain became angry (the first time the Bible uses the term) and "his face was downcast" (v. 5).

God wanted nothing more than to help Cain, and so he

instructed him not to be angry or depressed. He reminded Cain that blessing would come if he'd commit himself to doing right, and then the Almighty warned, "If you do not do what is right, sin is crouching at your door; it desires to have you, but you must rule over it" (v. 7). It was a dire warning, but Cain didn't take it to heart. He turned his back on God's instruction, turned his mind over to the sin crouching at his door. Cain invited his brother into the field, and there he dispatched him in cold blood.

If you look at the passage closely, the instrument of murder used by Cain is never mentioned. Was it a rock? A club? A well-honed knife? The Bible doesn't say. (It certainly wasn't a gun because gunpowder didn't come along until the ninth century.) To be plainer, it doesn't really matter. After all, the instrument of murder matters less than the motive underlying it. And what was that motive? Hate inspired by the evil one.

John, the most beloved follower of King Jesus, said as much. In a letter to the early church, he wrote of both the origins of murder and the antidote for it:

> For this is the message you heard from the beginning: We should love one another. Do not be like Cain, who belonged to the evil one and murdered his brother. And why did he murder him? Because his own actions were evil and his brother's were righteous. (1 John 3:11–12)

See the problem? It ain't the guns or the knives or the sticks or the stones. It's not even the violent movies or vicious video games or the fact that some dudes had a bad day or that someone didn't get enough love from his momma. Murder comes from a condition of the heart, a condition that is influenced by the evil one himself. It's demonic. But if a man gives himself to the love of the King, his hate-filled, murderous heart will be replaced with a heart full of the King's love.

King Jesus knew the truth about murder, and he cautioned his followers to root out all demonically inspired anger. In the Sermon on the Mount, he taught, "You have heard that it was said to the people long ago, 'You shall not murder, and anyone who murders will be subject to judgment.' But I tell you anyone who is angry with a brother or sister will be subject to judgment" (Matt. 5:21–22).

There's that word again: *anger*.

The murder problem that's plaguing America (the one that's been plaguing humanity since forever) isn't a gun problem; it's an anger problem, a hate problem, a lack-of-love problem. It's a spiritual health problem. And so long as we're mired in anger, hate, and malice, we'll have chaos in our schools and in our streets. We'll have continuing murder, whether by AR-15s, shotguns, knives, clubs, rocks, or ropes. (As an aside, you don't hear anyone arguing for increased rock restrictions, do you?)

Yes, there's only one solution for the current mass-murder problem in America. We have to return to the principles of the King. Where he reigns, murder has no place. Where his love is celebrated, death meets its demise. Put another way, when the love rate is high, the murder rate is low.

THE MANIFESTO IN ACTION: THE JESUS POLITICS OF GUNS AND LOVE

It is my firm, well-studied, river-rat reasoned opinion that removing firearms from the hands of the people will not remove hate from their hearts. What's more, removing those firearms might lead to a creeping tyranny, to a government whose power is no longer restrained by the power of its own people. So it's my estimation that advancing gun-control measures is creating a problem we've never had (tyranny) without solving a problem we've always had (murder in our hearts).

According to a Pew Research poll, 30 percent of Americans own a gun and 11 percent live in a gun-owning home.[6] That means there are roughly ninety-eight million gun owners in America. And of those ninety-eight million gun owners, how many have committed a mass shooting in 2018? Less than one thousandth of 1 percent. I know hundreds of gun owners, and I've spoken to thousands over the years. Many of them are Christian men and women, and though they're well-armed, it's never crossed their minds to walk into a school and shoot up the joint. They've never considered using a firearm for illegal purposes. And most never would. Why? Because as citizens of the kingdom, those gun owners are ruled by the law of love.

The solution for America's gun-violence crisis is to return to the King's law, the law of love. But how do we do that? Consider the following steps:

- Instead of promoting new gun legislation, promote the love of the King; preach it to the world around you.
- Vote for politicians who advance the King's love, too, knowing that's the only solution for America's murder problem.
- Promote policies that protect the Founding Fathers' wisdom that saw gun ownership as a right and a way to defend our freedoms (as well as our neighbors) from a government opposed to the King.

- Hold the line on the law of love, and if enough of us do, we might see a country that remains free enough to experience the love that casts out all fear, anger, hate, and malice (Eph. 4:31).

So whether it's this political season or any other one, don't be persuaded by the godless politicians and mainstream media who believe they can bring gun violence to an end without addressing the heart of the matter. Don't fall for their promises of peace and prosperity without a return to the King. Don't place your trust in political solutions. Place your trust in Jesus Politics and in the heart change only he can bring. Promote politicians who understand Jesus Politics, who know the solution to America's murder problem lies in the human heart and who promote spiritual solutions. Vote in line with the Founding Fathers and the King. And as you use your vote and your voice accordingly, realize you're protecting this country from a future of creeping godless tyranny.

A KINGDOM MANIFESTO

THE PROBLEM:

The mainstream media and politicians blame guns for the increasing levels of violence in America instead of addressing the true problem: hate in the human heart.

THE MANIFESTO OF THE KING:

We must address the hate in our hearts with the love of the King while preserving our right to bear arms against tyrannical governments.

A MANIFESTO IN ACTION:

Vote for leaders who seek to preserve gun rights while offering kingdom-based solutions to the anger that's tearing this country apart.

CHAPTER 5

On Biblical Environmentalism

If you've watched my shows, read my books, or sat across the table and chowed down on a stack of my Louisiana-famous Robertson-family hamburgers, there's one thing you know: I pride myself on being UnPhiltered. I speak my mind. I preach the truth. I run the outboard motor on my Jon Boat wide open. I fire at will and eat what I kill. What you see is what you get.

It's an honest way of living, living unPhiltered, but not everyone's on board. Not everyone appreciates my candor. Especially not the yuppie dudes and millennial gals who run the internet. Case in point: the fine folks at Facebook.

In 2017 I was promoting a new show on CRTV, a conservative internet channel now owned by BlazeTV. The show was called *In the Woods with Phil* and was meant to be an unPhiltered look into the ways I lived, the things I cooked, the animals I hunted, and my views on the Word of God. In preparation for that show, a small film crew followed me around my property after a morning hunt. I had my quarry—a couple of Green-winged Teal ducks—and I was prepping them for the gumbo pot. As I plucked the ducks, I offered a little commentary about the environmentalists who attack me with some regularity. I shared about how some folks say I shouldn't be out there killing animals, that I was a coward for murdering a helpless bird.

So I said, "It doesn't take a coward to kill a duck. It takes someone who is hungry, and he wants organic food out in the wild. You want organic? Follow me around. You can call me Mr. Organic."

Organic. That's me. I shared how over the years I'd taken most of my sustenance from the rivers and woods. Fish, deer, ducks, crawfish, plums, persimmons, dewberries, blackberries, mayhaws, sloes—that's what has made up the majority of my diet for most of my life. Yes sir, I've eaten organic all my life, and I haven't once set foot in the town square farmer's market. I've harvested them with my own two hands from the land given to me by the Almighty.

After singeing off the remainder of the feathers, I picked up the duck and showed it to the camera.

"Look out! He's got a face," I said. "There's a mouth. Eyes. Nose holes!"

And that's when I put his neck on the chopping block and separated his head from his body with a cleaver.

The video was edited and uploaded to Facebook in hopes that it might generate a little buzz for *In the Woods with Phil* and, boy, did it ever generate buzz. Turns out, Facebook doesn't appreciate the meat-preparation process, and they censored the video for "graphic violence or gore." I hadn't shot a gun on that video. I didn't blow anything up. Didn't kill anything on camera. I simply showed how harvest meat gets from the wilderness to the table.

Plucking a duck for the cooking pot is violent? Huh?

Six months later I got crossways with the Facebook camp again. This time, I was cleaning a mess of catfish for a fish fry. I demonstrated the cleaning process with one of the bigger fish, clipped his fins, skinned him, gutted him, and fileted him. My sidekick and redneck butler, Dan, was with me, and as I worked, we discussed how to use every part of the fish. The filets—we'd eat 'em. The guts and fins—we'd throw them in the crawfish traps as chum. It was a sort of day-in-the-life video, one that showed how we're dependent on the quarry the river gives us and how we don't take that for granted.

The folks at *In the Woods* uploaded the video to Facebook, and for the second time the social media company took issue with the video. Again the video was censored, slapped with a graphic content warning. Maybe it was because all the young'uns on social media got their undies in a wad over a little fish blood. Maybe it was because I was a conservative. Whatever the reason, it left me shaking my head and asking a simple question.

Men and women on Facebook, where do you think your meat comes from? You know it all has to be slaughtered, don't you?

It was free speech censored by a new version of The Man, a corporate media version with its own sort of agenda. But I didn't get upset about this kind of censoring of free speech, though I suppose I should have. Instead, I saw it for what it was: a group of self-ascribed progressive folks trying their best to silence biblical environmentalists, the ones who see the creation as a gift from the Almighty to humankind.

Here's the ironic part. Mark Zuckerburg and his allegedly environmentally conscious friends claim that if we don't address climate change, if we don't reduce carbon emissions from SUVs and private planes, if we don't quit piping coal ash into the air, if we don't cut back on methane emissions from cattle feed lots, we'll destroy the planet, maybe even in the next twelve years. (Can you believe they're even taking on cow flatulence?) But how do they spread the message? Jet-setting around the globe on private planes and yachts. Creating social networks that require historic amounts of energy, energy that has to come from somewhere. Driving from event to event in electric-powered vehicles charged by fossil-fuel-burning power plants. Sounds really environmental.

I suppose the Facebook crowd and their ilk could learn a lesson or two about true environmentalism from a true environmentalist. A biblically based environmentalist. A kingdom-centered environmentalist. Who is that environmentalist?

Yours truly.

Now before you lose your lid, consider my track record. I don't jet-set around the country for pleasure, and I generally stay within a few miles of my home. (That said, I fly from time to time to share the gospel wherever the King allows.) I wager I burn fewer fossil fuels in a year than the Zuckerberg camp burns in a month. I work to cultivate the land, try my best to create a desirable food plot for the winter duck migration. And I hunt those ducks, but only for sixty days out of the year, and I only take what will feed my family and friends. I do not kill without purpose. I never waste meat. I do not rape the land.

The new environmentalists talk a good game about saving the earth from the coming destruction. They love to spout off about the environment. But let's be honest. It's all part of their political game.

A GREEN BAD DEAL

If you're a student of-isms, you know America is no stranger to certain kinds of socialism. In the 1930s, at the height of the Great Depression, President Franklin D. Roosevelt used socialized government programs to pull the country out of the slump. He called that program the New Deal. With taxpayer money, American workers were employed by the federal government to build bridges, dams, roads, hospitals, government buildings, and the like. And I suppose, depending on which historian you listen to, it might have worked. (Some argue that cuts in spending, taxes, and regulation after World War II had more to do with pulling the country out of the Depression, and though I'm not a bona fide historian, I tend to agree with this assessment.[1])

The New Deal was a socialist set of programs celebrated to this day by left-wingers. So is it any surprise that in 2019 the current leftists proposed their own version of the New Deal? They called it the Green New Deal, and it was meant to operate as a new kind of kick start to the economy aimed at addressing climate change while creating new jobs. At least, that's what the young, up-and-coming politicians claimed, such as democratic socialist Alexandria Ocasio-Cortez.

What are some of the programs suggested by the Green New Deal? Consider this partial list collected by a mainstream media outlet:

- Meeting 100 percent of the power demand in the United States through clean, renewable, and zero-emission energy sources

- Building or upgrading to energy-efficient, distributed, and so-called smart power grids and working to ensure affordable access to electricity
- Upgrading all existing buildings in the country and building new buildings to achieve maximum energy efficiency, water efficiency, safety, affordability, comfort, and durability, including electrification
- Overhauling all the transportation systems in the country to eliminate pollution and greenhouse gas emissions from the transportation sector as much as is technologically feasible, including investment in (1) zero-emission vehicle infrastructure and manufacturing, (2) clean, affordable, and accessible public transportation, and (3) high-speed rail
- Working collaboratively with farmers and ranchers to eliminate pollution and greenhouse gas emissions from the agricultural sector as much as is technologically feasible[2]

Is the Green New Deal feasible, though? A Fox Business article cited a study released by the Competitive Enterprise Institute and Power the Future that concluded the effects of the proposed program would be less than positive:

At best, it can be described as an overwhelmingly expensive proposal reliant on technologies that have not yet been invented. Carbon—whether contained in wood, coal, gas, or oil—is a byproduct of burning fuel. Eliminating these energy sources would have massive ramifications for the economy.[3]

What kind of ramifications? Try tacking on costs to the

American taxpayer in the amount of somewhere around $93 trillion.[4]

Sounds like a bad new deal if you ask me.

The cost to American taxpayers was one thing. But then there was the hypocrisy of it all. After the Green New Deal was proposed, the media discovered Ocasio-Cortez didn't seem to care too much about the environmental impact of her campaign. Her staffers ran up the miles on their cars, even though there was a train station just a few feet from her office in Queens. There were over a thousand car-service miles attributed to her campaign. A news outlet reported, "Instead of embracing cheaper, greener travel methods, Ocasio-Cortez logged 66 airline transactions during her 2018 campaign while only using Amtrak 18 times."[5] Turns out, the queen of green was burning down the world.

It's odd to me, really. Hollywood and New York City are packed with environmental advocates. They talk a big game, tell us the world's going to hell, that it'll all turn to ash and cinder if we don't spend trillions of dollars to make it right. They question whether it's responsible to have children in a world that's burning up. They whine about using plastic straws. And yet these same politicians, actors, and environmentalists don't live by the green policies they promote.

Humanistic environmentalism is all fine and good as long as it suits their lifestyle, as long as it gives them a way to exercise power.

And this is the problem with the environmental movement as I see it. It's a man-made, fear-based-ism, one that elevates the power of humans over the power of God and his coming kingdom. But is there an environmental policy that's in line with the King?

You bet there is.

The Christian Response: Worship the Creator Instead of the Creation

There is an environmental policy that lines up with the King's view of creation. But before digging into the policy particulars, let's start at the beginning. Let's start with an examination of the heavens and the earth.

In the beginning God created the heavens and the earth, and as the psalmist wrote, "He set the earth on its foundations; it can never be moved" (Psalm 104:5). Then, just after the creation of the earth, the King made the sun, and the earth orbited around it. But the foundations of the earth—the North and South Poles—were not set to be equal distances away from the sun. Instead, the earth's axis was tilted ever so slightly. And as I've come to understand it, it's this tilt that's set the conditions for creation to flourish.

There are planets with no axial tilt, namely, Mercury, Venus, and Jupiter. There are some with extreme degrees of axial tilt, such as Uranus. Unlike these planets, though, the earth's axial tilt is slight, sitting at precisely 23.5 degrees. And this tilt accounts for the earth's weather and the changing seasons. Because of this tilt, there are times in the earth's orbit when West Monroe is closer to the sun. This accounts for our sweltering summers. As the earth moves around the sun, as it reaches the opposite side of the orbit, the same 23.5-degree tilt ensures West Monroe is just a little bit farther from the sun. This brings winter's edge, and with it the migration of the ducks I love to harvest.[6] But what if the earth were tilted a few degrees one way or the other? Well, life as we know it might not exist on Planet Earth.

Some scientists believe that if a world lacked weather (that is, if there were no tilt), areas farther away from the Northern and Southern Hemispheres would be plagued by a near-constant winter. Without the relief of spring and summer, there'd be less land to cultivate and most of the human race would be squeezed into areas closer to the equator. What's more, without the winter freeze in regions that could be cultivated, insect populations would run rampant, which might lead to damaged crops and more diseases. In other words, without the tilt, the earth would be an exercise in apocalyptic living for the human race.

Of course, it's not just the tilt of the earth's axis that makes our planet inhabitable. We've been given water, which comes in handy around duck-hunting season. Our earth is the perfect distance from the sun, which makes plant and animal life possible. (Again, making duck season a fruitful endeavor.) The Almighty has set the conditions for an inhabitable world. And what the Creator set in motion, his creation cannot stop. We cannot knock the world off its axis, can't shake it from its foundations. So what kind of arrogance possesses us to think we could destroy the thing God so precisely made for us?

God created a precise ecosystem for us and all his creation. This being the case, we ought to ask ourselves why.

In the beginning, God created the rivers, the woods, and the fields—a veritable garden—and he put man and woman smack in the middle of it. Our charge was simple: work the earth and take care of it (Gen. 2:15). The Almighty gave us charge and dominion over the earth, made us to "rule over the fish in the sea and the birds in the sky, over the livestock and all the wild animals, and over all the creatures that move along the ground" (1:26). Then the Almighty gave us "every seed-bearing plant on the face of the whole earth and every tree that has fruit with seed in it" (v. 29) as a food supply.

"Hold on just a second," my vegan readers might be saying. "See how the Almighty created man to be vegetarian?"

Not so fast, Mr. Vegan.

After the great flood in Noah's day, the Almighty opened up the food chain. He said to the survivors who'd been protected by the giant boat, "Everything that lives and moves about will be food for you. Just as I gave you the green plants, I now give you everything" (Gen. 9:3). With that verse, we got new orders from headquarters: meat is in. If it walks, crawls, flies, or swims, we can whack it and stack it. Skin it and fin it. Grill it. Roast it. Deep fat fry it. Eat it up.

Yes, the Almighty made us stewards of the earth. He gave us freedom to cultivate it and eat from it. He gave us freedom to hunt the animals too. And he did all of it for our enjoyment. He did it so we'd remember his goodness.

The Scriptures are clear about the purpose of the environment. In the book of Hebrews, the writer begins a run on faith with a statement about creation: "By faith we understand that the universe was formed at God's command, so that what is seen was not made out of what was visible" (11:3). In the book of Romans, Paul wrote: "For since the creation of the world God's invisible qualities—his eternal power and divine nature—have been clearly seen, being understood from what has been made, so that people are without excuse" (1:20). See? Everything in creation was meant to point us to the Creator.

Everything? you ask.

Everything, I say.

Cucumbers, tomatoes, and onions?

Mix 'em in a salad bowl and tell me they aren't the work of the Almighty.

Mallards and teal?

You ever eat a duck gumbo, dude?

What about oil or petroleum?

Consider how God created gasoline for our cars, how he allows us to use it for transportation. Consider how gasoline has been used to spread the gospel.

King Jesus knew the purpose of creation better than any of us, knew how it could be used as a point of connection with the Almighty. Jesus himself took to nature to hear from God. On more than one occasion he withdrew to the wilderness, the desert, or a mountain to connect with his Father in prayer. He used nature as a teaching tool too. In the Sermon on the Mount, he pointed to the birds and the flowers, told us not to worry about what we'd eat or wear because we'd be fed and clothed better than fowls and flora (Matt. 6:25–29). In the parable of the sower, he used creation to show how the kingdom of God grows:

> As he was scattering the seed, some fell along the path, and the birds came and ate it up. Some fell on rocky places, where it did not have much soil. It sprang up quickly, because the soil was shallow. But when the sun came up, the plants were scorched, and they withered because they had no root. Other seed fell among thorns, which grew up and choked the plants. Still other seed fell on good soil, where it produced a crop—a hundred, sixty or thirty times what was sown. Whoever has ears, let them hear. (Matt. 13:4–9)

Jesus, the Word of creation incarnate, used the natural world to point us to the King.

All of creation is meant to point us to the King, to teach us about the King, and to spread the news of his kingdom. This much is true. But from the beginning, lawless people have elevated the creation over the Creator. They've worshipped Mother Nature instead of Father God. Don't believe me? Paul said as much: "Although [humankind] claimed to be wise, they became fools and exchanged the glory of the immortal God for images made to look like a mortal human being and birds and animals and reptiles" (Rom. 1:22–23). What was the result of this exchange?

> Therefore God gave them over in their sinful desires of their hearts to sexual impurity for the degrading of their bodies with one another. They exchanged the truth about God for a lie, and worshiped and served created things rather than the Creator— who is forever praised. (vv. 24–25)

See there? When we worship the creation over the Creator, we're wading into troubled waters.

And listen up millennial environmentalists; worship of the creation is a dead end. Why? Because if you think climate change is bad, just wait till the judgment of the King comes. The apostle Peter, the one who'd been given the keys to the kingdom, described that event:

> But the day of the Lord will come like a thief. The heavens will disappear with a roar; the elements will be destroyed by fire, and the earth and everything done in it will be laid bare.
>
> Since everything will be destroyed in this way, what kind of people ought you to be? You ought to live holy and godly lives as you look forward to the day of God and speed its coming. That day will bring about the destruction of the heavens by fire,

and the elements will melt in the heat. But in keeping with his promise we are looking forward to a new heaven and a new earth, where righteousness dwells. (2 Peter 3:10–13)

The elements will be destroyed by fire. See there, global warming is a biblical guarantee. But if you worship the King, if you honor him above the environment, you'll experience something even better than what we have here, namely, a new and perfect earth with the city of God at its center. What will that city look like? In the book of Revelation, John shared:

Then I saw "a new heaven and a new earth," for the first heaven and the first earth had passed away, and there was no longer any sea. I saw the Holy City, the new Jerusalem, coming down out of heaven from God, prepared as a bride beautifully dressed for her husband. And I heard a loud voice from the throne saying, "Look! God's dwelling place is now among the people, and he will dwell with them. They will be his people, and God himself will be with them and be their God. 'He will wipe every tear from their eyes. There will be no more death' or mourning or crying or pain, for the old order of things has passed away."

He who was seated on the throne said, "I am making everything new!" (21:1–5)

He continued in the following chapter:

Then the angel showed me the river of the water of life, as clear as crystal, flowing from the throne of God and of the Lamb down the middle of the great street of the city. On each side of the river stood the tree of life, bearing twelve crops of fruit, yielding its fruit every month. And the leaves of the tree are for the healing of the nations. No longer will there be any curse. The throne of God and of the Lamb will be in the city, and his servants will serve him. They will see his face, and his name will be on their foreheads. There will be no more night. They will not need the light of a lamp or the light of the sun, for the Lord God will give them light. And they will reign for ever and ever. (22:1–5)

Imagine the new earth and the city of God in it: crystal-clear water, a tree of life bearing not one but twelve crops worth of fruit, no death, no night, a place where kingdom citizens reign forever and ever with the King. Doesn't that sound so much better than the world we're trying to save? It does to me.

THE MANIFESTO IN ACTION: THE JESUS POLITICS OF THE ENVIRONMENT

You don't have to be a river rat like me to adopt a Jesus Politics worldview as it relates to the environment. You don't have to spend hours a day outdoors or harvest all your food from the land. The environment is God's gift to us, river rats and city slickers alike. So no matter where you make your home, pay attention to the sunrise that takes your breath away. Consider the roar of the ocean on your family vacation or take in the beauty of your nearest national park. Recall how awe-inspiring it is to see a muskrat, a deer, or a flock of mallards in the wild. The call of creation is a call to worship the Almighty if we'll let it be. But if we worship the creation instead of the Creator, our end will be no different than the end of nature itself: total destruction.

Now listen, I'm not saying green energy is bad. I'm not knocking solar power or electric cars or windmills. You want to drive around in an electric go-cart a full-grown man can't fit into? Go for it, dude. I'll support you. What I am saying, though, is to have a little common sense. Don't be bamboozled by the Chicken Little politicians who claim the sky is falling, who claim only they have the solution. Don't vote for those who'd squander billions of dollars to protect plants and animals the Almighty already cares for. Don't spend so much energy saving the environment that you miss the Creator of that environment in the first place.

So, as a citizen of the kingdom, how should you approach the environment with Jesus Politics? Consider:

- Voting for politicians and policies that advance biblical environmentalism, that is, environmentalism that protects our God-given rights to cultivate, hunt, and use private land for the glory of the Almighty
- Shutting down the policies of environment worshippers, people who'd prioritize Mother Earth over Father God
- Doing your part to enjoy nature, using it to direct your attention and the attention of others to the Almighty

If you do these things, if you live by the principles of biblical environmentalism—even if it's a simple act like thanking God for a beautiful sunrise, taking a walk in the woods, saying grace over a vine-ripened tomato, or simply trusting that God cares more for his creation than you do—you'll find great peace and tranquility as you commune with the King in his garden. (Just as Jesus did on the mountainside.) You might also find yourself inviting others to recognize and enjoy the goodness of God's creation, drawing

— A KINGDOM MANIFESTO —

THE PROBLEM:
Modern politicians have advanced a new
form of environmentalism that worships
the creation over the Creator.

THE MANIFESTO OF THE KING:
It's time to be kingdom environmentalists,
stewards of the land who cultivate, grow,
harvest crops and animals, and use the other
resources of the earth all to the glory of God.

A MANIFESTO IN ACTION:
Vote for leaders who elevate the Creator over
creation, who don't use environmental hype
to create fear in order to procure power.

CHAPTER 6

On Life According to the King

By now, you know my story. I was a heathen, a depraved pagan who loved booze, drugs, women, and ZZ Top (in no particular order). I was a bar-owning brawler, a man with little regard for the lives of others and even less regard for the law. I'd never met a vow I wouldn't break, including the vows to my wife. Buck wild as I was, though, there were some things I'd never contemplate, things beyond the depths of my redneck depravity. Among them: abortion.

When I rose from the waters of baptism into the kingdom of heaven in 1976, abortion had been legalized by the United States Supreme Court for only three years. But concerned as I was with leaving my sinful ways, repairing my relationship with Miss Kay, and learning to be a productive member of society, I remained oblivious to the genocide happening on American soil. In fact, it wasn't until I asked Miss Kay to get me the party platforms that I began to give abortion a second thought. It wasn't until I reviewed those platforms that I began to understand how left-wing politicians were using the political process to pave the way for a culture of death.

Political observation opened my eyes. And now, around sixty million abortions later, I'm more aware than ever. Aware of the continuing slaughter of children. Aware of how the Enemy uses political power to perpetuate this insanity. And the insanity seems to be getting worse.

On January 22, 2019, a government under the complete influence of the evil one advanced the policies of death. The New York state legislature had gathered to present a bill to Governor Andrew M. Cuomo. It was the forty-sixth anniversary of *Roe v. Wade*, the Supreme Court decision that legitimated abortion, and though it was a day we should all mourn, the abortion advocates of that day were celebrating. They'd passed a death bill, which they called the Reproductive Health Act. Through it, the legislators meant to protect a New Yorker's right to terminate a pregnancy (I marvel at the ways we dress up the language of death), including abortions during the third trimester of gestation and maybe even up to the day of delivery. Now, they'd gathered with the governor to sign the bill into law.

Cuomo took to the podium before signing the bill, and he delivered a speech meant to excite the crowd. He defended the law on partisan grounds, said it was necessary to protect the people of the state from the Trump administration's attempts to roll back abortion rights across the country. Wearing a slick suit and a pink tie, he called the moment bittersweet.

The death of babies is bittersweet?

"Today is sweet," he said, "because in a few minutes, I will sign this bill, and another New York national precedent will be

established, [namely,] the most aggressive women's equality platform in the nation is going to be a law in this state."[1]

*Equality for all women except those little women who might
be terminated in the womb, that is. Right, Governor?*

He continued: "There is a bitterness, because we shouldn't
be here in the first place. We should not have a federal government that is trying to roll back women's rights to a point 47, 48,
50 years ago. This administration defies American evolution.
We're supposed to be moving forward, we're supposed to be
advancing, we're supposed to live and learn, we're supposed to
be growing."[2]

*We're all supposed to be growing, except those babies in the
wombs. Right, Governor?*

Cuomo then passed the microphone to an abortion rights
advocate. Moments later, the governor moved to a desk, scribbled
his name on the bill, and before the ink had dried on his signature, he declared, "Congratulations! The bill is signed!"

The crowd erupted in applause.

It was the worst of government actions, a state-sanctioned
excuse for the taking of human lives. It was a declaration that
lives do not matter, particularly when those lives are confined to
the womb. And it would have been bad enough had that been the
only abortion scandal that month. But it wasn't.

Only one week later, another governor argued in favor of
even farther-reaching abortion rights. Virginia governor Ralph
S. Northam was reportedly considering a law that would make
it easier for women to obtain late-term abortions. The governor
was being interviewed live on the radio, and he was asked about
a proposed bill in the state legislature and how it would protect

third-trimester abortions. A pediatric neurologist by occupation, he said this about late-term abortions:

> It's done in cases where there may be severe deformities, there may be a fetus that's nonviable. So in this particular example, if a mother is in labor, I can tell you exactly what would happen. The infant would be delivered. The infant would be kept comfortable. The infant would be resuscitated if that's what the mother and the family desired, and then a discussion would ensue between the physicians and the mother.[3]

Discussions? About what? Whether to terminate a resuscitated baby outside the womb because it has some deformity?

I don't pretend to know exactly what Governor Northam meant. It's hard to crawl into the head of someone who refuses to bow his knee to King Jesus. But this much I know: the governor's comments evidence a lack of regard for life. Should a baby's potential be snuffed out because it might have a deformity? No way.

He who lacks regard for life, especially innocent life, lacks regard for King Jesus, the giver of all life, the one who holds all life together (John 1:3–4; Col. 1:16–17). Make no mistake about it, Jesus Politics demands the followers of the King fight for all innocent life.

LIFE: THE KING'S DEFINITION

In 1973, the Supreme Court put itself in the seat of the King, deciding what constitutes human life. In *Roe v. Wade*, the

Court declared, "The word 'person,' as used in the Fourteenth Amendment, does not include the unborn."[4] A kicking, punching, moving human with a heartbeat, brain activity, and the ability to feel pain was not a person simply because it hadn't been born? Does this make a lick of sense?

Come on now, Your Honors.

I'm no lawyer, and I haven't been trained in the hallowed halls of Harvard or Yale. I've risen to the top of my class here on the river, though, and I've learned a thing or two about the moment when life begins. And really, it's not that hard a concept to grasp, so listen up. Life begins when any living being—tree, flower, egg-encased embryo, or otherwise—takes up space. Consider the following river rat's simple example.

In *The Theft of America's Soul*, I wrote about the miracle of life on this planet, how it's continued on and on over thousands of years. There, I recalled moments spent with my sons in the woods, how I picked up an acorn of a mighty oak and passed it to one of the boys. I pointed to that tree and described that so much life sprang from that small seed. But how could we know when such a small acorn transformed into something more than just a seed, into something living? Simple. Look at the ground. See the green pushing up out of the hull, rooting down into the Louisiana mud. Was it tiny, particularly when compared to its father oak? Yes. Was it vulnerable to wind, rain, and the hoof of a passing deer? Sure. Still, did that tiny green sprout take up space? No doubt. And would anyone argue the sapling was not alive? Not anyone with a lick of logic. In fact, by my own observations, I suspect the Greenpeacers of the world would agree.

Shouldn't the logic of the tree apply to human life? When a man and a woman come together, when they lie together and bring their unique offerings together in love, something amazing happens. One tiny sperm finds one tiny egg. *Bang!* One tiny embryo forms. The seedling of human life. And in that moment, a new being begins taking up space in the woman's womb.

This rapidly dividing, rapidly growing embryo? Is it life? I suppose if it were an oak tree, there'd be no doubt. And there's no doubt in the mind of the Almighty about human life either. In fact, as far as he's concerned, life begins even *before* conception. He said as much to the prophet Jeremiah:

> The word of the LORD came to me, saying,
> "Before I formed you in the womb I knew you,
> before you were born I set you apart;
> I appointed you as a prophet to the nations." (1:5)

And if Jeremiah would have been conceived these days, if he were an unwanted pregnancy, do you think God would have gone the extra mile to protect his prophet? It's a hypothetical, I know. But I suspect he would have.

From the earliest stages, every embryo has the unique capacity to be a person known by God. Named by God. Called by God to a unique task. Even before the newborn takes its first breath. And King Jesus wants to know and love each human life. The Scriptures share as much.

JESUS ON THE WORTH OF A CHILD'S LIFE

This seedling of human life grows and grows, and then nine months later comes wailing into the world. That newborn, the same baby that took up space in the mother's womb, takes up space outside the womb and grows and grows and, over time, comes to walk, talk, and reason. What started as nothing more than a seedling becomes a full-sized child. To understand the value of that life, we need look no further than to the very life of King Jesus himself.

King Jesus, the firstborn of all creation, came into the womb of an unmarried woman (without any need for sex with a man, for what it's worth). He began his life as an embryo, and over nine months he grew in that womb. The King of kings and Lord of lords came to take up space in Mary, and when the time was right, he left that womb and entered the world. From embryo to baby boy. From childhood to adulthood. This was the journey of God with Us. And though he never spoke about abortion directly (maybe because the idea would have been unthinkable to anyone in his day), he made no bones about the worth of the life of a child.

King Jesus was what you might call a pretty big deal. But though the King could have spent time with the important people of the day, though he could have demanded attention from kings, dignitaries, and religious leaders, he didn't. Instead, he spent time with those viewed as the least among the people: fishermen, tax collectors, blind, lame, poor, outcasts, and the children.

In the Gospels, Jesus makes much of children. Matthew, Mark, and Luke each record a similar story. Parents brought their children to Jesus and asked him to lay hands on them and pray for them. In each story, the disciples (the King's own men) tried to turn the people away, thinking the children were too trivial a matter for Jesus. Seeing their attempts to keep the children from him, Jesus became indignant. Put another way, he was as mad as a hornet. He chastised his disciples and said, "Let the little children come to me, and do not hinder them, for the kingdom of God belongs to such as these" (Mark 10:14 NIV; Luke 18:16; Matt. 19:14).

In the gospel of Matthew, the disciples came to Jesus and asked who'd be the greatest in his heavenly kingdom? Was it Peter, the fisher of men? John, the beloved disciple? Maybe it was Mary, his mother. Turning the tables (a thing Jesus was prone to do), he pulled a child into his lap and answered:

> Truly I tell you, unless you change and become like little children, you will never enter the kingdom of heaven. Therefore, whoever takes the lowly position of this child is the greatest in the kingdom of heaven. And whoever welcomes one such child in my name welcomes me. (Matt. 18:3–5)

Welcoming a child is like welcoming the King?

If the disciples were slow on the uptake, the religious leaders were even slower. In the days before his execution, as Jesus entered Jerusalem, children gathered in the temple courts and shouted, "Hosanna to the Son of David." The Scriptures indicate the chief priests and teachers were spitting mad, and they asked, "Do you hear what these children are saying?"

"Yes," Jesus said and then asked, "Have you never read, 'From the lips of children and infants you, Lord, have called forth your praise'?" (Matt. 21:15–16).

See. Even infants praise the King. And if I had my guess, I'd suspect he meant infants in the womb too.

Jesus valued children, the little people of simple faith who always believed, always loved, always praised, and always ran to the King. Their innocence made them the greatest in the kingdom of heaven. And what kind of logic says the greatness of their innocence only begins the day they're born? What kind of logic denies them this dignity while God is forming them in the womb? Do you think King Jesus would snuff out their lives in the womb?

The evil one isn't so much concerned with the logic of life, though. In fact, he's hell-bent on stealing, killing, and destroying all life, especially the lives of children, the greatest in the Almighty's kingdom (John 10:10; Matt. 18:1–5). Satan has worked his way into American politics, has done his best to perpetuate the genocide of the unborn. And if Jesus were walking around Washington or New York or Hollywood today, he might say exactly what he said to the religious leaders of his day: "You belong to your father, the devil, and you want to carry out your father's desires. He was a murderer from the beginning, not holding to the truth, for there is no truth in him. When he lies, he speaks his native language, for he is a liar and the father of lies" (John 8:44).

HOW CITIZENS OF THE KINGDOM PROTECT LIFE

King Jesus feels so strongly about children that he calls them the greatest in the kingdom. Do you think he'd support ending those lives before they had an opportunity to sit in his lap?

No way, Governor Cuomo.

No way, New York.

No way, Governor Northam.

There's not a doubt in my mind: Jesus—the one who knows us

in the womb, the one who gives us light and life—wants nothing more than for all human life to be protected. And as people of the kingdom, we're supposed to value the things valued by our King. We're to love the people he'd love and protect the ones he'd protect, including unborn babies in their mothers' wombs. We're to make the King's desires known to our elected officials and demand and direct them in the way of preserving the dignity of unborn human life too. We're to use our votes to put people in office who will work to end this awful American genocide. And where our political action is ineffective, we're to use our time, money, and influence to persuade others to protect life. Just as Miss Kay does.

If ever there were a woman dedicated to ending abortion, it's Miss Kay. With great regularity, she meets with women who've fallen on hard times, women who sometimes find themselves just out of prison, down and out, sometimes addicted to drugs, and, on occasion, pregnant. Time and time again, she counsels those who turn up pregnant to visit Life Choices Pregnancy Resource Center in Monroe, a place that offers hope to unexpected mothers. Her reputation for choosing life is well known in the community, so well known, in fact, that she often receives calls from friends of friends asking whether she'll intervene in the life of a mother who's considering abortion. Just a few weeks ago, Miss Kay told me about one such story.

On a typical Sunday afternoon, she received a call from a friend, a manager at a retail department store who'd overheard two women talking. One told the other she was pregnant, that it was unexpected. There was no support, the woman said. No money. No father to take care of the baby. And she was considering an abortion.

Miss Kay asked her friend to put the phone down and open up a conversation with the woman and invite her to visit Life Choices. The manager did just what Miss Kay asked, and a few minutes later picked up the line and asked Miss Kay to meet her at the resource center in thirty minutes.

Miss Kay hung up the phone and called Life Choices and found out they were getting ready to close for the day. Robertsons don't take no for an answer when it comes to human life, so Miss Kay told the woman on the line that closing wasn't an option. A life was on the line, and she expected a counselor who could perform an ultrasound to be there when she showed up in a few minutes. The woman at the center agreed and said she'd find a tech as soon as she could, and she'd be waiting for the pregnant woman and Miss Kay. So Miss Kay grabbed her keys and headed to town.

Sure enough, the manager and expectant mom showed up at Life Choices shortly after Miss Kay arrived there. The pregnant woman shared her story, shared her fear and confusion. Miss Kay and the folks at the center assured her there were resources available to help her carry the baby to term and keep the baby. And if she didn't want to keep the baby, there were people who would love to adopt a newborn. The woman listened and agreed to an ultrasound, and they all heard the heartbeat. And that was that. The woman made up her mind. How could she execute something with a heartbeat?

A citizen of the kingdom had overheard a conversation influenced by the evil one and sprang to action. The result was one less life added to the genocide census; one more life given the opportunity to commune with the Almighty. It was grassroots action, action that upheld the values of the King. And in this political climate, it was subversive action, one that flew in the face of lawmakers in Washington DC, New York, Virginia, and across the country.

So in this political and social climate where unborn life is not valued, how can the citizens of the kingdom take a more proactive approach to protecting life? How can we use Jesus Politics to advance King Jesus' agenda for life? Consider being proactive. Consider taking these actions:

- Vote for men and women who'll fight against America's culture of death and for judges who are inclined to do the same.
- Picket, protest, and speak out against government-sanctioned death, whether at the federal level, the state level, or in your community.
- Get involved in grassroots action and support your local crisis pregnancy center.

It's time to use our voices, our feet, and our hands. It's time to take the fight for life to the evil one on his turf and carry the truth of the King as our weapon. That's what the store manager did. It's what Miss Kay did too. The people at Life Choices do it every day. And if we adopt Jesus Politics, particularly as it relates to the value and dignity of human life, we'll do the same.

——— A KINGDOM MANIFESTO ———

THE PROBLEM:
American politics perpetrates the
genocide of the unborn.

THE MANIFESTO OF THE KING:
Life must be protected from the
very point of conception.

A MANIFESTO IN ACTION:
Vote for leaders who advance the policies of life, the
policies of the King, and look for opportunities to serve
women with unexpected or unwanted pregnancies
with the truth from the King for their circumstances.

————————— **CHAPTER 7**

For the American Family

I was raised in a different day and age. A time you might describe as more primitive. Fathers were real men with rough hands, and they worked hard to support the family. They were handy and knew how to use a full belt of tools. They mended fences to hold the livestock, built barns for the animals, and helped their neighbors do the same. Mothers were the matriarchs of the house. They cooked the meals, fed and milked the cows, and taught the children during the day. Kids, for the most part, were to be seen and not heard, at least when it came to offering any guff about the chores that needed doing. We were taught to respect our parents, teachers, preachers, police officers, and judges and to do our best to follow the Almighty. And if we didn't? If we got out of line? It was a rough day for our hindquarters.

Primitive. That's the way to put it. And not just because we followed a simple order for the family and for society. It was primitive in so many ways.

We lived in rural Louisiana, and by all measures we were dirt-poor. When we weren't tending the animals, I ran around barefoot with my six brothers and sisters in the yard, the field, the barns, wherever we could find space to play. But all that running around barefoot comes with certain risks. Among them? Roundworm infestation. And so, once a year, my mother dipped into the family savings and called the doctor, who came out to the house to administer a little white pill. A foul-tasting dewormer.

Now here's the truth, and it might not come as any surprise to you: I've had a rebellious streak since I came out of the womb. A touch of lawlessness. And round about my tenth year of living, the doc came to deliver and administer the dewormer to my siblings and me. We gathered in the living room and stood in a line, hands out and waiting to receive our yearly dose, which we swallowed without water. I hated those pills worse than anything, and so, after the doctor placed the pill in my hand, I waited until no one was looking, and I tossed it over my shoulder. I went through a charade and pretended to swallow that medicine. Where'd the pill go when I tossed it to the wind? I didn't know and I didn't much care. I'd pulled a fast one and gotten away with it. Or so I thought.

Weeks later my mother was cleaning behind the stove, and she swept up that little white pill. Mom called the doctor, and when he arrived, she lined us all back up. She showed us that pill and asked who hadn't taken theirs. I knew it was mine, but if I didn't confess, what could go wrong? After all, she couldn't punish me if she couldn't pin it on me. Right?

Wrong, young Phil.

The doctor went down the line, handing out another round of medicine. He placed the pill in each child's hand and stood there, watching to make sure each of us put it in our mouths and swallowed it. And after we'd gotten it down the hatch, Mom followed up behind us and issued some medicine of her own. A couple of good old-fashioned swats with a paddle. All seven of us took our pills and a paddling that day, and one by one we were dismissed to the yard.

In the yard, my four older siblings peppered the rest of us with questions, and it wasn't long before they'd pieced it together. I was the cheat. The sneak. The liar. I was the one who'd been responsible for the second dose of medicine and the group swats. And it was time for me to take a second set of licks, this time from my righteously indignant older siblings.

Resistance was futile, and I took my lumps that afternoon, both from my mother and from the elder Robertson kids. If that would have been all, it'd have been enough. But evidently my siblings ratted me out to my mother, who ratted me out to my father. And when he came home that night, he took a turn at meting out justice. Could he have let the whippings from my mom and siblings stand? Sure. But that wasn't his way. Instead, he whupped me for both lying and requiring the doctor to come out for a second call. Doctors weren't cheap, he reminded me. And we didn't have any extra money lying around, he also reminded me.

It wasn't always the easiest way to grow up, especially if you had a rebellious streak in you. But, still, there was a natural order to the family in those days, an order that kept us in line for the most part. My father and mother were at the top, and they answered only to the Almighty. All the children were subject to parental authority, but the older Robertson kids helped to enforce my parents' rule of law too. And it was this way of being that ensured the survival of the Robertson camp. In fact, it was this rule of law that kept me from getting into too much trouble while I lived under my parents' roof.

When I got out on my own, I denied the family structure my parents hoped to instill in me. I didn't give a lick about the King or the ways he'd instructed his people to operate. I didn't care to be the head of my family or to partner with Miss Kay in bringing up godly children under my roof. Instead, I wanted to party and leave Miss Kay to raise the children. I was more interested in flirting and carousing with any woman who crossed my path. I denied the godly order of family and what did I get for it?

A wife who left me.

Children who didn't know me.

A life that was tearing apart at the seams.

Miss Kay could have divorced me, could have thrown me to the wolves. She didn't, though. Instead, she prayed for me, and when I realized how miserable I was, when I asked her to take me back, she first took me to the preacher, Bill Smith. He helped me to see how broken my life was, how wrecked I was with sin. He shared the good news of King Jesus with me. I followed Christ into the waters of baptism and was introduced to a group of men who taught me what the Bible had to say about becoming a man of God. I'm happy to say I learned how to be a godly husband to Miss Kay, who took me back. I learned to love, honor, and lead Miss Kay the way the Bible teaches and how to partner with her to raise up our children. I learned how to discipline my children and teach them the good news of the Almighty. I learned the power of embedding our family in the local church.

All these years later, I can attest to the benefits of raising a family the way God intended. Miss Kay and I love each other and like to spend time together. My four boys love the Lord and do their level best to follow him. They're loving husbands and fathers too, and they've trained their kids in the way they should go. What's the result? The Robertson camp is happy, happy, happy.

THE PROBLEM: HOW AMERICAN POLITICS CHANGED THE FAMILY

The 1960s was an era when professors and politicians declared God was dead and tried to bring about a humanist society. Those were the days of debauchery and hippie living. Those were the days when the American family came under attack. I know. I was there. In fact, even though I didn't buy into the humanist philosophy per se, I was all in on the debauchery.

It was a raucous time full of good music (some of the best guitar pickers ever born came out of the sixties) and bad thinking. And with the rise of godless teaching in high schools and colleges, with the rise of free love, drugs, and rock and roll, the moral foundations of America began to crack. Our desires led us away from the biblical teachings about sex and the family, and we began empowering politicians who'd give us what we wanted: a shifting of the roles of men and women, freer sex, and easier ways to dissolve our marriages. America was in a cultural shift if not a cultural crisis, and as that shift took hold, the state of California introduced the first no-fault divorce legislation. Before this no-fault divorce law, divorce was granted only if one party committed adultery, abandoned the other, or committed a terrible felony. But for the first time in American history, the folks on the Left Coast declared marriage could be terminated by either party for no reason at all.

What sprang from the California brain trust spread to every other state in America, and by 2010 every state had some version of no-fault divorce in place. The results? Whereas before the 1950s the divorce rate was less than 20 percent, by the mid-1970s almost half of all marriages ended in divorce.[1] That rate of divorce has come down somewhat over the years, but a recent *Time* magazine article indicated, "Experts now put your chances of uncoupling at about 39% in the U.S."[2]

Uncoupling—ain't that a fancy word for *divorce*?

I'm no social scientist or psychologist, but I know this much: divorce has serious effects on the fabric of our country. It disrupts God's plan, leaving children without a stable mother-father relationship. It destabilizes the loving and instructional environment God intended for children. It often leaves them torn between a mother and father at odds, between two parents who can't agree on what's best physically, spiritually, or emotionally for the child. Researchers have noted that children from divorced homes suffer academically, are more likely to be incarcerated for committing a crime as a juvenile, are more likely to live in poverty, and are more likely to engage in underage drinking, drug abuse, and risky sexual behavior.[3]

But do you think these issues only plague the children of divorce in their youth? Is it possible those same problems follow our kids later in life?

Just look around, America.

And if it were only the sky-high rate of divorce that put the American family in jeopardy, that'd be one thing. But it's not. In 2015, the Supreme Court redefined marriage altogether, claiming that marriage was no longer limited to a relationship between a man and a woman. With its decision that marriage was a fundamental right for same-sex couples, the highest court in the land opened up the floodgates. And now, in this age of easy divorce and same-sex marriage, what constitutes a family? It might be a single mother raising a slew of kids with no father in sight. (And on some occasions this might be warranted.) It might mean a father raising children without a loving and nurturing mother. (And, yes, there might be good reasons for this too.) A family might consist of two men raising a daughter or two women raising a son. The word *family* defies definition and order these days, and we have our godless politicians to thank for this relatively modern experiment.

There is, however, a simple and undeniable truth. Though the American definition of *family* might be in flux, the Word of God is unchanging. The definition of *family* according to King Jesus and his Word trumps any new definition coming out of Washington, DC. But what does Jesus Politics have to say about the family?

THE CHRISTIAN RESPONSE: WHAT KIND OF FAMILY DID THE KING CREATE?

In the beginning, the Almighty made a man and named him Adam. God placed Adam in the garden and set the man to work by naming the animals and tending the soil. But plants and animals weren't company enough for Adam, and when God saw how lonely he was, the Almighty decided to give him a companion, a helper. Eve. A woman. And together Adam and Eve kept each other company. They did such a good job at keeping each other company, in fact, that Eve became pregnant with their firstborn, Cain. And then again with their second, Abel.

Man and woman partnered together and brought children into the world. As the Bible records, "That is why a man leaves his father and mother and is united to his wife, and they become one flesh" (Gen. 2:24).

Man and woman were told to be fruitful and multiply, to bear children and populate the earth. And that's exactly what they did and what their children's children did. But having children and raising them isn't just an obligation. It's meant to be a joy. As the psalmist wrote, "Children are a heritage from the LORD, the fruit of the womb a reward" (127:3 ESV).

The family—a father and a mother raising children in the way of the Almighty—was the design, and it was meant for the good of society. And knowing us better than we know ourselves, knowing we needed order, the Almighty gave each of us distinct roles in that family unit. What were those roles?

Husbands are to love their wives "as their own bodies. He who loves his wife loves himself. After all, no one ever hated their own body, but they feed and care for their body, just as Christ does the church" (Eph. 5:28–30).

Wives are to "submit yourselves to your own husbands as you do to the Lord. For the husband is the head of the wife as Christ is head of the church, his body, of which he is the savior" (vv. 22–23). And as an aside, if a husband loves his wife well, this kind of submission shouldn't be burdensome or difficult. Why? Because your husband will consider your opinions, thoughts, gifts, and unique contributions. He'll prize those things above all others.

Parents are placed over the children and tasked with teaching them about the Almighty "when you sit at home and when you walk along the road, when you lie down and when you get up" (Deut. 11:19). Parents are to mete out discipline to their children too. As the Scriptures attest, "Whoever spares the rod hates their children, but the one who loves their children is careful to discipline them" (Prov. 13:24).

And what is the child's place in the order? It couldn't be more straightforward. "Honor your father and your mother, so that you may live long in the land the LORD your God is giving you" (Ex. 20:12). Children are to honor the Almighty by honoring their parents.

There is a natural order to all this, see, and God created that order for our benefit. In that order, husbands love their wives, wives love their husbands, parents love their children, and children love and honor their parents. It's an order that brings stability to a family. In fact, researchers have found that married couples tend to live longer, have better relationships with their children, and their children tend to be healthier.[4]

If we obeyed God's order—one man and one wife loving and submitting to each other and teaching, instructing, and disciplining their children in the Lord—our families would thrive. Just like mine and Miss Kay's. And this shouldn't come as any surprise. After all, the King's ways are much higher than our own.

WHAT DID KING JESUS TEACH ABOUT THE FAMILY?

King Jesus made his thoughts on the family known. In Matthew 19, the teachers of the law had asked whether divorce was proper. He could've given them a straightforward answer, a yes or a no. Instead, he went back to the beginning, back to the Almighty's intention for marriage. He said:

At the beginning the Creator "made them male and female," and said, "For this reason a man will leave his father and mother and be united to his wife, and the two will become one flesh." . . . Therefore what God has joined together, let no one separate. (vv. 4–6)

The lawmakers didn't like his answer, and they asked why Moses allowed the people of Israel to divorce if the Almighty was opposed to it. Jesus answered them, "Moses permitted you to divorce your wives because your hearts were hard. But it was not this way from the beginning" (v. 8).

Jesus didn't just talk about marriage, though. He taught about the role of children too. He taught that children should honor their father and mother, even into adulthood. Speaking to a group of religious leaders, he said, "Whoever speaks evil of father or mother must surely die" (Matt. 15:4 NRSV). But Jesus taught this kind of honor extended well after the child left the home and extended beyond honoring parents with words. Honoring parents included providing for them materially as they aged. He indicated as much, teaching that the practice at the time of dedicating property to the Lord instead of using it to care for elderly parents was offensive and that it made "void the word of God" (Matt. 15:1–9 ESV).

See, from the beginning, the Almighty had a plan in mind, a plan King Jesus affirmed. And it was that plan that would create stable family units and, in turn, a stable society. Those families would give birth to other kingdom-centered families. And through the proliferation of these sorts of King-honoring family units, the love of the King would spread throughout the world. The kingdom would come on earth as it is in heaven.

But what about those who'd rather not take a member of the

opposite sex for a spouse? What about those who aren't attracted to the opposite sex or would rather not marry and raise children? (Jesus said there'd be eunuchs among us, which I take to mean folks who wouldn't get hitched up with a member of the opposite sex.) Does that mean you have no family responsibilities? No way. Jesus, who was God in the flesh, took no wife himself, but he spoke directly of the kingdom family. The gospel of Mark reported it this way:

> A crowd was sitting around [Jesus], and they told him, "Your mother and brothers are outside looking for you."
>
> "Who are my mother and my brothers?" he asked.
>
> Then he looked at those seated in a circle around him and said, "Here are my mother and my brothers! Whoever does God's will is my brother and sister and mother." (3:31–35)

Paul, a devout follower of King Jesus who gave us the majority of the New Testament, was unmarried, and he devoted his singleness to the glory of God. He worked tirelessly to spread the gospel of Christ, and he encouraged others to stay unmarried if they'd do the same so long as they could control their desires. To the people of Corinth, he wrote, "To the unmarried and the widows I say: It is good for them to stay unmarried, as I do. But if they cannot control themselves, they should marry, for it is better to marry than to burn with passion" (1 Cor. 7:8–9).

Followers of the Almighty, we're all in the family and we all have familial duties. We're all responsible to support the family structure ordained by God, all responsible to teach and train the children, all responsible to come together in a larger family that worships the King. And with that comes a certain kind of responsibility, namely, the responsibility to speak up for the Almighty's family structure in every facet of our lives, including in the political arena.

AS FOR ME AND MY REDNECK FAMILY, WE WILL SERVE THE LORD

In 2012, *Duck Dynasty*—a show about our God-fearing, gun-toting, redneck family—swept Middle America. We owned our time slot and had millions of viewers. Over eleven seasons, we drew viewers from across the country, particularly from the South and the Midwest, that so-called flyover portion of the country that so many politicians talk about these days. We were unconventional for a television family. We didn't cuss or drink. We prayed on television. We spoke about God openly. We loved each other and lived out God's intention for family as best we could. And as we did, our popularity only rose.

I can't exactly say why *Duck Dynasty* was so popular, but I have an educated guess. I reckon the American people were waiting to see a functional family they could identify with, maybe even aspire to. They wanted to see men who were godly men, who worked hard, played hard, taught the gospel in every facet of their lives, and weren't mocked at every turn by their wives. They wanted to see godly women who honored God, cared for their family and community, and were loved by their husbands. It gave them hope to see children respecting their parents (at least for the most part) and living lives of intentional faith. The American people needed to believe the God-centered family was still important to American life.

We've done our best to create the kind of family the Almighty honors. One man, loving one wife, raising children to love, honor, and serve the King. It's an atypical family structure in America these days, one the politicians (which is to say nothing about Hollywood) seem determined to destroy. Still, we've reaped the benefits of it, such as peace, prosperity, and a family in which every member knows they're loved.

THE MANIFESTO IN ACTION: DEFEND GOD'S PLAN FOR THE FAMILY

The godless politics of men can't change the family structure set forth by the Almighty, no matter how hard they try. But if they keep undermining God's design, America will continue to suffer the consequences as a country. What consequences?

A lack of discipline.

Increased violence.

Increased rates of depression.

A country of godless, senseless, loveless, self-absorbed, self-indulgent, uncommitted people.

Sound like the kind of country you want to live in? Not me. So as you're considering which political candidates to vote for and which policies to support, ask yourself whether they're aligned with the family values of the King. Ask yourself:

- Which political candidate does their best to love and honor their spouse?
- Which political candidate has well-behaved, God-honoring children?
- Do the candidates believe in the biblical view of marriage, ensuring that children are raised with a mother *and* a father?

- Who will advance the policies that support traditional family values, even if they don't live them out perfectly?
- Who will protect your right to teach the younger generation the ways of the Almighty and to discipline them when they step out of line?

And if there's no perfect candidate (there never is these days), ask yourself, *At the very minimum, who won't get in the way of applying Jesus Politics as it relates to the family?* Then, march into the public square and declare the Almighty's truth about the family. Support organizations that advocate traditional, biblical views of marriage. Finally, walk into the voter booth and prayerfully cast your vote in a way that aligns with the King, blesses the citizens of the kingdom, and promotes the King's family design for all humankind. Then rest knowing that when you protect the American family, you're protecting America herself.

——— *A KINGDOM MANIFESTO* ———

THE PROBLEM:
American politics endorses policies that
disrupt the Almighty's original plan for family,
which undermines a stable society.

THE MANIFESTO OF THE KING:
Citizens of the kingdom must protect, preserve,
and promote the Almighty's view of marriage:
one man married to one woman and raising
their children to love and serve the Lord.

A MANIFESTO IN ACTION:
Vote for leaders who cling to the biblical view
of the family and promote policies designed to
strengthen families rather than destroy them. Then
promote the organizations that do the same.

CHAPTER 8

For Kingdom-Centered Healthcare

I was reared in the 1950s in a rural home. There were nine of us in the Robertson camp in those days, and as I shared in the previous chapter, our access to healthcare was limited. Maybe even more limited than the average American family. We lived miles outside of town in a log cabin some might call rudimentary, and aside from the yearly worm medication, we tended to our own ailments for the most part. We had no health insurance. Not many did in those days. No way to pay for regular doctor's visits. Instead, we relied on simple remedies. A bottle of milk of magnesia for heartburn and constipation. A little Mercurochrome or Dr. Tichenor's for a skinned knee. Tape for a cut that wouldn't close up. Folk remedies for everything else. And for the most part, if those simple remedies wouldn't fix what ailed us, we were told to toughen up.

Sure, there were times when milk of magnesia or Mercurochrome or tape wouldn't do. There are some injuries no amount of toughening up would fix. And in those instances, Mom would load us up and haul us to the clinic. There, the doctor would tend to the wound or the broken limb. And when he was finished, he'd charge us a buck and send us on our way. There was no paperwork. Very little hassle.

We couldn't afford to take medical care for granted in those days, and neither could our neighbors. If someone had an infection or a cold or injured themselves, the community pulled together and helped out where they could. (Remember the story of my dad's injury from chapter 1?) A good neighbor might bring a homemade poultice or salve or some chicken soup to the house to help speed up the healing process. They might tend to their neighbor's garden or livestock or fishing nets for a day or two if a particularly rough bout of influenza came around. Neighbors helped neighbors in times of hardship. I guess you could say the community was the safety net when the worst illnesses hit, and we were both recipients of and participants in that safety net.

I was a pretty hard-boned kid, and my immune system was firing on all cylinders, so I made my way through childhood without too many visits to the doctor and without much need for the community safety net. I graduated from high school, married Miss Kay, and moved on to college without any thought of buying health insurance. Sure, we visited the doctor and hospital from time to time when Miss Kay was pregnant, but it was still affordable. And truth be told, outside of the birth of our kids, we didn't have much use for the medical community. Between our home remedies and the kindness of our neighbors, we got along just fine. But while we were accustomed to making it with more rudimentary healthcare practices, the attitude in the country was changing.

In 1965, President Lyndon B. Johnson signed laws creating Medicare and Medicaid, a system of medical insurance that covered the poor, disabled, and elderly. Through the 1970s more and more employers began offering health insurance, and as they did, folks in this country began to see healthcare as a necessity, one right up there with food, clothing, and shelter. The healthcare industry took note, and prices for treatment began to rise.

By the 1980s the politicians in Washington recognized just how American thinking about healthcare had changed, how everyone wanted access to some kind of health insurance. They'd noticed the rising costs of healthcare too. And as I awoke to what was happening with politics, I noted how politicians used the people's changing attitudes toward healthcare to leverage their own political power. I noticed how they began using promises of healthcare as a carrot.

By the early 1990s the idea of healthcare as a universal right had taken hold in some of the more left-leaning pockets of America. In 1993, First Lady Hillary Clinton presented a healthcare bill that would have required every American to get some kind of health insurance coverage. Under Clinton's plan, the government could force you to part with your hard-earned dollars to purchase insurance you might never use (especially if you were a Robertson river rat). It was a garbage idea, and Congress wasted little time in shooting it down.

The leftists lost the battle to require government-mandated healthcare, but did that keep most of the politicians from trying to ramrod it through? No way, dude. Just seventeen years later, President Barack Obama took a second stab at it, and this time the leftists got their way. Obamacare was born in all its glory, requiring every citizen to buy health insurance, whether through their employer or on a government-facilitated exchange. With this new law, we took one step closer to becoming a full-blown nanny state. And because those plans were as expensive as all get-out, more and more Americans called for universal government-provided healthcare.

See how socialism creeps up on you?

In 2018, a mainstream media outlet reported:

> The vast majority of Americans, 70 percent, now support Medicare-for-all, otherwise known as single-payer health care, according to a new Reuters survey. That includes 85 percent of Democrats and 52 percent of Republicans. Only 20 percent of Americans say they outright oppose the idea.[1]

This idea of healthcare as a universal right is pretty recent. Old-timers like me remember a day and age when it would have been laughable. So answer me this, America: When did we begin to feel a sense of entitlement to free healthcare? Is it possible it came from good motives, that it was a well-meaning attempt to fight the war on poverty? You bet. Is it possible, though, that it was nothing more than a political position used to get votes?

I don't have to answer that, do I?

Politicians these days love to trot out the promise of free healthcare. As the 2020 presidential debates began, Senators Bernie Sanders, Cory Booker, and Elizabeth Warren and Mayor Pete Buttigieg all supported some kind of Medicare-for-all system. The remainder of the serious Democratic candidates supported further government intervention in the healthcare system.[2] And, yes, I understand that everyone needs healthcare from time to time, and it might seem like a godly idea to provide healthcare for those in need. But is it the government's place to provide that healthcare? If you believe it is, answer me this: How can a universal healthcare system serve so many people's individual needs without infringing on their religious rights? I'll tell you: it can't.

THE PROBLEM: WHO WILL YOU TRUST?

Healthcare as a universal right is the rallying cry of the age. Healthcare is the issue of the day, the one that pulls at the heartstrings of the American people and the suit jackets of all the politicians in Washington. And as the debates go on, I've noticed a curious thing: though once rugged, self-sufficient, and suspicious of big government, the American people now want to place their healthcare in the hands of big government instead of in the hands of God.

Thomas Jefferson was right when he said the people in this country had the right to pursue life, liberty, and happiness and that the government should preserve and protect that right. There's a difference, though, between protecting and preserving our rights and giving us everything we want. And rest assured, any want met by the government will come with strings attached. (More on that later.) What's more, the government can't fix the most pressing of all human healthcare concerns: we're all headed toward the grave.

As followers of the King, we know there's no human system that will fix our biggest healthcare concern. Every form of treatment on this earth is a stopgap, a half measure. And don't get me wrong, I'm glad we have doctors and surgeons and other professionals who can help us out when we're sick, broken, or come down with some disease. After all, we have an obligation to be good stewards of our own well-being. But there's only one healthcare plan that gives us what we really want, and that's the eternal healthcare plan the King has already laid out for us. How do we gain access to this eternal healthcare plan? Let's take it one step at a time.

King Jesus, the eternal Word of God, knew the sinful ways of lawless men and women. He knew human sin created a barrier between us and God, and that because of sin, each of us would be subject to disease, death, and ultimately the judgment. And so he came down from heaven and walked among us, living a perfect and sin-free life. At the end of his ministry, he offered himself in a great exchange, giving himself to the political authorities—Jews and Romans alike—and suffering an unjust death on a cross to pay for our sins. Quoting the prophet Isaiah, the apostle Peter laid out the effect of Christ's crucifixion: "'He himself bore our sins' in his body on the cross, so that we might die to sins and live for righteousness; 'by his wounds you have been healed'" (1 Peter 2:24).

Healed from what? From spiritual disease, the disease that doesn't just infect our bodies but our souls. But it's not just spiritual disease he came to heal us from, and before you think I'm selling some sort of faith-healing mumbo jumbo, think again. The kind of physical healing Jesus brought might not be what you think.

After Jesus' death, he was laid in a tomb for three days. At the end of those three days, he conquered death, rising in a perfected body. He walked around in that body for a few weeks, spending time with his disciples before returning to heaven. The apostle Paul recorded that truth:

What I received I passed on to you as of first importance: that Christ died for our sins according to the Scriptures, that he was buried, that he was raised on the third day according to the Scriptures, and that he appeared to Cephas, and then to the Twelve. (1 Cor. 15:3–5)

What impact does his death and resurrection have on our physical bodies? (Hold on to your hat, son.) Paul made it plain:

But Christ has indeed been raised from the dead, the firstfruits of those who have fallen asleep. For since death came through a man, the resurrection of the dead comes also through a man. For as in Adam all die, so in Christ all will be made alive. (vv. 20–22)

See there? Christ doesn't just offer forgiveness of sins and freedom from guilt and shame. He offers a way to beat physical death and the grave, to raise to new life with a new and incorruptible body. Now there's something the politicians in Washington, DC could never give you.

Freedom from sin, shame, and death? Resurrection from the grave? Could you have dreamed up such promises? Not me, dude. And this is why I've put my faith in Christ's eternal healthcare plan, the only healthcare plan that guarantees freedom from sin and shame, resurrection from the grave, and an eternity of disease-free living. This is why I preach it everywhere I go.

The way I see it, America, it all comes down to this. Who are you going to put your trust in? Are you going to place your health in the hands of a bunch of bureaucrats with no medical experience, who have no plan to foot the bill, and who cannot

109

solve your most pressing healthcare concern (death), or will you place your health in the hands of the King of kings, the Lord Jesus who can save you from the grave and raise you to eternal health?

Seems like a no-brainer if you ask me.

WHAT'S WRONG WITH TRUSTING GOVERNMENT HEALTHCARE?

This is all fine and good, you might say, but aren't there still some very real medical care needs in America in the here and now? Can you really turn a blind eye to the millions who can't afford healthcare?

It's a fair question. And listen, I'm not saying there aren't people who need very real help in today's society. But for the follower of Jesus Politics, the answer should never be to hand that responsibility over to the government. Why? Because in this day and age of increasingly godless government, any sort of government-run healthcare is going to come with a few godless strings attached. What do I mean?

In 2014, Miss Kay, Al, and Lisa visited the headquarters of Hobby Lobby to speak to the good folks there. The Green family owns Hobby Lobby—a Christ-centered business that sells arts and crafts supplies across the United States—and had been friendly to our family over the years and wanted to hear more about the Robertson family's prolife work. And while they were there, they shared some war stories. Miss Kay shared about her prolife work here in Louisiana, and the Greens shared their trials and tribulations as they tried to live out prolife Jesus Politics in their Oklahoma-based company.

After Obamacare became the law of the land, new government regulations required Hobby Lobby's private plan to cover the costs of certain kinds of pills for its employees, pills that killed a fertilized embryo after sex. (You may have heard of these so-called morning-after pills.) Hobby Lobby, a company owned by committed Christians, didn't take well to the mandate, seeing those pills as another form of abortion. So what did they do? They stood up to what they considered godless behavior and refused to comply with the requirement and filed a lawsuit against the government.

The case made its way through the court system and went all the way to the Supreme Court. The Court ultimately ruled that a family-owned corporation with deeply held religious beliefs, such as Hobby Lobby, could refuse to provide access to certain forms of contraception through their health insurance plan. The company celebrated the victory, though they saw it as a close call. The decision was a one-vote victory. If only one of the justices had voted differently, the Greens' case would have gone the other way.

Miss Kay told me their story, which I had some familiarity with through the news, although I hadn't appreciated all the details.

I said, "I'll bet this is only the beginning. Before long, I'll bet companies are required to cover abortions through government healthcare."

Miss Kay said, "I'll bet you're right, Phil. And I'd bet that'll be the case in our lifetime."

And herein lies the problem. For now, the Supreme Court has declared the government can't require a family-held business—such as Hobby Lobby or Duck Commander—to provide abortion healthcare services. But what happens when they change their minds? Even more to the point, what happens when the citizens of this country finally vote for some kind of government-run healthcare-for-all sort of system? You think they'll be any restrictions on women gaining access to morning-after pills or even abortions? I doubt it. And who will foot the bill for those abortions? That's right. The taxpayers.

So many in the government have a clear agenda, and it's one they aren't hiding. They want to take over the healthcare system and tax the people to make it happen. Use those tax dollars to provide services that are not healthcare services at all, but rather services that destroy life. And as this sort of godless nanny state becomes normalized, we'll lose sight of the only one who can give us life to the full: King Jesus.

THE MANIFESTO IN ACTION: SO WHAT ARE WE TO DO?

As citizens of the King, as followers of Jesus Politics, we need to be clear. We need to share how government-run healthcare is just a front for the taxpayers' funding of immoral behavior. We need to share about eternal healthcare everywhere we go. We need to show the people that what they ultimately want—a solution for pain and death—can only be found in King Jesus.

As we speak out, we need to be proactive too. We need to help our neighbors as we can, help foot a medical bill here and there. Our churches ought to reach into the community and care for the sick. After all, it was King Jesus who said we ought to love our neighbors as ourselves (Mark 12:30–31). It was King Jesus who said that as we serve the down and out, we serve him (Matt. 25:45).

So if you see your neighbor hurting, if you know of his healthcare needs, meet them as best you can. If enough of us did that, if we meet the needs of one another, there will be no need for government healthcare. And don't you think the watching world would take notice? Don't you think it'd make us true ambassadors for the Almighty?

So as citizens of the kingdom, let's advance Jesus Politics. Consider the following:

- Vote for those who will keep the government out of the medical system so they cannot advance a godless agenda (including requiring taxpayer funding of abortions or morning-after pills).
- Support politicians and policies that fight for a free-market healthcare system, the only kind of system that will be responsive to the paying public.
- Preach the importance of eternal healthcare everywhere you go.
- Get involved at the grassroots level, helping your neighbor when a medical need arises.

America, let's trust the right entity for our healthcare, the only one who can save us from sin, shame, death, and disease. Let's go all in on his eternal healthcare plan and invite our neighbors to participate with us. And let's call this movement for socialized medicine what it is: a scheme to get American Christians to foot the bill for death.

A KINGDOM MANIFESTO

THE PROBLEM:
Politicians hope to convince us to put our trust in the American government instead of God, tempting us with the idea that government-funded healthcare is not only good for everyone but also a right of every citizen.

THE MANIFESTO OF THE KING:
Resist government healthcare systems that advance godless procedures, rob you of hard-earned money, and don't provide the solution to your biggest need, namely, spiritual health.

A MANIFESTO IN ACTION:
Vote for leaders who protect the medical system from godless politicians and get involved in your community to help provide for the medical needs of those around you.

CHAPTER 9

Of Mercy and Forgiveness

The year 2019 was a busy year. Fuller than a deer tick in the summer. Faster than a duck on a june bug. I was just over a year into my program for BlazeTV, *In the Woods with Phil*. I'd just released my first book in a number of years, *The Theft of America's Soul*. And if that weren't enough, Al, Jase, and I were hosting a new podcast, *Unashamed*, which was also recorded and hosted on BlazeTV. I was seventy-three years old, and I was pursuing the kingdom harder than ever. And with these three different endeavors to promote, I found myself smack in the middle of New York City on what someone called a publicity tour.

A publicity tour in New York City? If my parents could see me now, they'd keel over laughing.

Our wives had traveled along (boys, don't leave home without your Bible and your wife), and so we decided to stay in the best accommodations we could afford. We decided to stay at the

115

Trump International Hotel. Even a river rat has to treat his wife to a little indulgence every now and then.

On our first morning in New York, we met in the lobby, and as we waited for the driver, Jase said, "This is the first time I've stayed in this hotel since they kicked me out. Remember that, Dad?"

Boy did I. Years earlier, the family had gone to New York City on a different kind of promotional tour. On the first night of that tour, Jase had booked a room at the hotel, and as he walked in, he asked a cordial staff member where the bathroom was. Now by all objective measures, Jase might be the scraggliest of our bunch, and without his wife, Missy, by his side, he must have looked completely out of place. If I had my guess, that particular employee of the Trump Hotel had watched his fair share of training videos and likely had plenty of experience with the homeless population of Manhattan. He knew just what to do when he saw Jase.

With a smile and a nod, the gentleman ushered Jase down a hallway. They went through one door. Then another. The polite employee opened a third door, and it wasn't until it closed behind Jase that it dawned on him. He'd been escorted out through the rear entrance of the building.

Jase walked back around to the front of the building and found us waiting in the lobby. He told us what happened.

"I think I just got kicked out."

We looked at him in disbelief and then he added, "I think it was a case of *facial* profiling."

The joke sent the whole family into an uproar. It was high comedy, the kind of stuff you couldn't make up, so when the cameras rolled on *Live with Kelly and Michael*, Jase led with the story. There was no animosity in the way he told it, no grudges.

He hadn't demanded an apology or made a fuss about it. In fact, he laughed it off with the rest of us. He'd forgiven the employee the minute he'd gotten the boot.

Back in those days, anything a Robertson did made the news, and the story of Jase being treated as a vagrant at the Trump hotel was no exception. But the story was made all the more significant by the fact that another celebrity—someone bigger than any of us—had been mistreated in a similar fashion. She'd been shopping in Europe when she was refused access to an almost $40,000 purse, allegedly being told she couldn't afford it. Did she let it go? Nah. She blew it up, made a big deal out of it.

And so when the news of Jase's hotel removal hit the news, there were two stories standing in stark contrast, and the bloggers and other media types took notice. One celebrity—Jase—had extended grace, mercy, and forgiveness for a misunderstanding when he'd been offended. The other had not.

I guess someone in the Trump organization must have been watching the television that morning, and word made its way to the top. A manager reached out to Jase and apologized for the misunderstanding. Jase took that in stride and told them he didn't harbor any anger or bitterness. It was all understandable, he said. And this response made it back to Donald Trump Jr., who called to thank Jase for his graciousness. And this is how the Robertson camp came to meet the Trump camp.

I listened to Jase tell the story, thinking about how his response had paved the way for my meeting with Donald Trump before he was elected in 2016. I considered how I'd been given the opportunity to share the saving message of Jesus with the future president, an opportunity that might not have ever happened had Jase thrown a tantrum in the lobby.

And as I considered it all, I asked, "Is it any wonder?"

Jase and Al looked at me, waiting for me to finish my thought.

"They've been so kind to you since you walked in, Jase. One of them even said, 'Welcome home.'"

It was a little example of the power of forgiveness, a funny story. But as I thought about it all years later, I considered how cultivating an attitude of mercy and forgiveness shapes our lives. It was a story that demonstrated how extending mercy and forgiveness leads to open doors and presents opportunities to share the good news of Jesus Christ. Forgiveness. Could forgiveness be the single most effective way of advancing Jesus Politics, particularly in such a vitriolic age?

THE PROBLEM: FORGIVENESS AND MERCY—A DISAPPEARING COMMODITY

Forgiveness and mercy are in short supply these days, especially when it comes to politics. The anger, name-calling, and stone-throwing seems to be at an all-time high. Few extend the benefit of the doubt anymore. It doesn't take a court of law to declare you guilty, and when you're convicted in the court of public opinion, you're dismissed and declared unworthy of mercy or forgiveness. And if you don't know what I mean, you aren't keeping up with the news.

In 2018, I watched as a nominee to the Supreme Court, Brett Kavanaugh, suffered through an attempted political assassination. Since he was a conservative federal judge, I expected the usual political wrangling. I figured those on the Left would raise his prolife record and might attack his stance on universal healthcare or the environment. I figured some would say he was too conservative, and they'd do their best to mar his reputation by picking over his judicial rulings. What didn't I expect? I didn't expect they'd dig up dirt from his high school days and try to use it against him.

That September, Christine Blasey Ford came forward with incredible accusations. She alleged Kavanaugh had locked her in a room and sexually assaulted her when both of them were in high school. Kavanaugh denied the allegations, saying they were a political hit by left-wingers. The media took sides, of course. Left-wing outlets attacked Kavanaugh and right-wing outlets attacked Blasey Ford. The commentators went nuts. They resorted to name-calling, finger-pointing, and character assassination. And all of this happened in the wide-open public because of an allegation of behavior that was supposed to have happened thirty-five years ago.

But it's not just the right-wingers who've suffered as a result of unforgiveness and a lack of mercy. Months later, in May 2019, Governor Ralph Northam of Virginia admitted that he was one of two men in a racist photograph taken thirty-five years earlier. He recanted his admission the following day, but it was too late for him to save face. The damage had been done. Again the political talk shows spooled up. Again they unleashed all manner of fury on him. Again Governor Northam was tried and convicted in the court of public opinion. And no one seemed willing to extend any sort of grace his way. No one in the media waited till all the facts came out, and no one asked whether he'd repented, whether he'd amended his ways and fought against racism throughout his political career. Instead, his youthful indiscretions were used as fuel for a current political fire.

Brett Kavanaugh was ultimately confirmed and now sits on the Supreme Court, and Ralph Northam is still in office. And to be clear, I make no claim as to whether these men are guilty or innocent of anything they've been accused of. I won't cast any aspersions at Blasey Ford, either. I only highlight these stories to show how the lack of mercy, grace, and forgiveness disrupts the political process and draws our attention away from the real issues plaguing our country.

I don't spend much time on the internet or social media, but I watch enough cable news to know the debate and dialogue out there is merciless. Politicians and constituents fight, cuss, and spit at one another, using the mistakes and sins of the past against others in order to gain political power. (And, yes, I'm aware President Trump regularly throws some low blows on social media.) Often, they don't give a rip about the facts. They believe the worst without extending an ounce of grace or understanding.

Have a skeleton in your closet from thirty years ago? You can guarantee your opponent will use it against you.

What if it's an unsubstantiated claim? They'll use that too.

Any mistake, misstatement, poor decision. Watch out, dude. It'll disrupt if not ruin your career.

Now don't get me wrong, if Justice Kavanaugh or any other politician broke the law, and if the evidence leads to a conviction and sentencing, then they ought to be held accountable. They ought to be removed from office and face the legal consequences for their crimes. But short of that, all this bickering and fighting isn't good for our country. Digging up thirty-five-year-old sins and blasting it across the media might make for good television, but what does it really accomplish? Does it help us solve any problems facing our country or does it only serve as a distraction from the issues that really matter? And so, America, the way I see it, we need a new way of speaking in the political arena. We need a new way of dealing with our political opponents. We need to act as Jesus would if he were engaged in our current political climate.

THE CHRISTIAN RESPONSE: THE FORGIVENESS AND MERCY OF KING JESUS

If you've followed me for any amount of time, you know I haven't lived the most spotless life. In fact, for the first two decades of my life, I was pretty unruly. So if you wanted to drag a skeleton out of my closet from all those years ago, it wouldn't take you long to find one. Truth be told, I've dragged out plenty of my own skeletons over the years in an effort to be honest about who I was before the Almighty got hold of me. But when I walked away from those years of lawlessness, when I walked into the saving work of the Almighty, I found a God who forgave every sin and dealt with me in great mercy. I found a church full of people who did the same, who didn't hold any of my past sins against me. Why were these people so forgiving? Why were they kind to me? They followed the way of King Jesus.

Forgiveness doesn't come to us naturally. It's something that's learned as it's experienced. To put it another way, to learn forgiveness, we have to be forgiven. And there's no better way to learn and experience forgiveness than to look at the life of King Jesus, the man who went to the cross to wipe away all our sins.

King Jesus could have put all his political foes to shame. He could have outed all their sins, even the hidden ones, and used it to climb the ranks of power. But God with Us came with a different purpose in mind. He came to forgive us, to free us from the sin and shame of everything we've done and everything we'll do. This is the good news of Jesus.

Each of the Gospels contains a story in which Jesus had been invited to dinner at some important person's house. There, a woman approached him, anointed his feet with perfume, and then wiped it off with her hair.

The gospel of Luke gives additional detail, though. The woman was a notorious sinner, and everyone in the community knew as much. She came to Jesus unannounced and fell to the ground, covering his feet with her tears, wiping them with her hair, and then dousing them in perfume. The Pharisee who invited Jesus thought that if Jesus were a real prophet, he'd surely know the woman was a sinner, and he'd keep her at arm's length. But Jesus read the Pharisee's mind, and he used it as a moment to teach on forgiveness. Luke recorded the conversation between Jesus and the Pharisee:

> "Two people owed money to a certain moneylender. One owed him five hundred denarii, and the other fifty. Neither of them had the money to pay him back, so he forgave the debts of both. Now which of them will love him more?"
>
> Simon [the Pharisee] replied, "I suppose the one who had the bigger debt forgiven."
>
> "You have judged correctly," Jesus said.
>
> Then he turned toward the woman and said to Simon, "Do you see this woman? I came into your house. You did not give me any water for my feet, but she wet my feet with her tears

and wiped them with her hair. You did not give me a kiss, but this woman, from the time I entered, has not stopped kissing my feet. You did not put oil on my head, but she has poured perfume on my feet. Therefore, I tell you, her many sins have been forgiven—as her great love has shown. But whoever has been forgiven little loves little."

Then Jesus said to her, "Your sins are forgiven." (7:41–48)

Time and time again, Jesus' ministry was marked by forgiveness and mercy, and he called others to extend that same forgiveness and mercy. Need proof? Consider these passages:

- In the Sermon on the Mount, Jesus warned the people: "For if you forgive men their trespasses, your heavenly Father will also forgive you. But if you do not forgive men their trespasses, neither will your Father forgive your trespasses" (Matt. 6:14–15 NKJV).
- When the religious leaders caught a woman in adultery, when they threatened to stone her on the spot, Jesus said, "Let any one of you who is without sin be the first to throw a stone at her" (John 8:7). Then he forgave her sins.
- When Peter asked how many times he ought to forgive the sins of his neighbor, when he offered "up to seven times?" Jesus responded. "Not seven times," he said, "but seventy-seven times" (Matt. 18:21–22).
- And what was one of Christ's last acts on the cross? He looked down on his opponents, the men who crucified him, and spoke these words over them: "Father, forgive them, for they do not know what they are doing" (Luke 23:34).

Jesus was not quick to cast stones. He didn't attack his opponents, political or otherwise. He didn't accuse the accusers. Instead, he extended forgiveness and grace to all.

Does this mean King Jesus let everything go, that he didn't take hard stands on the issues? Hardly. He didn't tolerate sin, and he preached some hard words about lust and anger and greed and gossip and the like. But time and time again, when the people fell short, Jesus picked them up, dusted them off, and forgave them, sometimes when they didn't even ask him to.

THE MANIFESTO IN ACTION: THE ROLE OF FORGIVENESS AND MERCY IN JESUS POLITICS

As followers of King Jesus, as citizens of the kingdom, we're called to be like him. Yes, we're to take a hard line on sin, debauchery, and lawlessness. We're to call folks in the world around us to repentance and invite them into kingdom living. But how do we do this? Not through name-calling or by lording the past over our opponents. Instead, we're to be quick to extend mercy and forgiveness, slow to judge. It won't always be easy, particularly when folks on the other side of the political spectrum try to drag us to the bottom of the barrel when they drag out the past of our political leaders in an attempt to destroy us. It won't be easy when we uncover decades-old dirt on our political opponents either, dirt that might give us an advantage in an upcoming election. But still, as followers of King Jesus, as citizens of the kingdom, we're to engage our opponents—including our political opponents—as he did. With mercy and forgiveness.

Now, don't hear what I'm not saying. Extending mercy and forgiveness to our political opponents doesn't mean there aren't consequences for sin, particularly sins committed by politicians while holding public office. If a sitting Supreme Court justice has broken the laws of the land, you'd better believe there should be consequences. If a president lies or obstructs justice while holding office (particularly if there's evidence to back up the claim), then he or she should be held accountable. Even, still, you can only dole out these consequences with a sober and forgiving spirit. You can remove a man from office without hate and vitriol. Ultimately, you can hope the consequences of his sin humble him and lead him to repentance. And if it does, the citizens of the King can be there, waiting, ready to show him mercy and lead him to the Almighty who removes every sin and every consequence.

So as you enter into political debate during an election cycle, discuss the issues plaguing our country. But as you do, ask yourself:

- Do I forgive those who represent opposing political viewpoints the way I'd want to be forgiven?
- Would I hold a politician's distant past against them in order to gain a political advantage?
- Do I speak with the same mercy and forgiveness I'd want my politicians to demonstrate?
- Do I demand that my leaders extend mercy and forgiveness to their political opponents, that they show civility in the way they carry out the day-to-day business of governing?

If the answer to these questions is no, do something about it. Refuse to attack a politician for his past shortcomings while

A KINGDOM MANIFESTO

THE PROBLEM:
American politics is eaten up with anger, hate, and
unforgiveness, distracting us from dealing with
the issues that really matter to our country.

THE MANIFESTO OF THE KING:
As you engage the political system, don't be
dragged down into a hate-filled quagmire.
Forgive political opponents as you've been
forgiven. Show them mercy as you've been shown
mercy, even as you debate their policies.

A MANIFESTO IN ACTION:
Don't get dragged into the political vitriol. Instead,
reflect the character of Jesus and extend grace
and forgiveness to those on the other side of the
political aisle. Demand the same of your politicians,
and pave the way for meaningful political debate
instead of continual partisan bickering.

PART II

SHARING JESUS POLITICS IN EVERYDAY LIFE

CHAPTER 10

The Law and Order of the King

I consider myself a keen observer, a man with a knack for noticing things. In the woods, I observe animal tracks, the way predators often follow the paw prints of prey down the river road. I notice pooling water and follow it back to the places the beavers have laid up their dams. I notice the tiny oak shoots in the woods, the sprouting millet in the spring fields, and the cuts in the river where the catfish hold.

As a hunter and fisherman, a lover of the great outdoors, I've been trained to observe. After all, if you don't pay attention to the signs of life, you'll never find your quarry. But my powers of observation are not simply relegated to the natural world. They extend to the human family too.

In 2017, I was preparing to launch *In the Woods with Phil*, and because it'd be on a conservative network, I figured it wouldn't be watched by too many folks on the other side of the political spectrum from me. So, though I knew I'd have an opportunity to share the good news of the Almighty with conservative viewers who might not be believers, a question set in. How could I reach more people with the gospel of Jesus? And as I considered it, another question hit me: Had I ever led a left-winger to Jesus?

I called Al and ran the question by him.

He said, "If you have, I can't remember it."

So I asked him, "What about you, Al? You ever led a liberal to Jesus?"

There was a long pause before he said, "I don't think I have."

This observation washed over me like floodwaters, and that's when the second question almost pushed me under.

Why not?

I held onto that observation for weeks, maybe even months. And then, on an episode of *In the Woods*, I shared it. I'd never led a politically left-leaning man or woman into the kingdom of heaven, at least not that I was aware of. Still, didn't I believe in God's grace? Didn't I believe he could break into a lawless person's heart and bring her into the love of the Almighty? He'd done it with me. So why hadn't I seen this kind of breakthrough with other lawless folks?

A year passed, and the question still plagued me. I kept asking Al why we hadn't led left-wingers to Jesus. I considered the question with my nephew Zach, who produces *In the Woods*. I asked Miss Kay about it, and she didn't have any answers either. But one afternoon in the summer of 2019, she brought me a letter that set me at ease.

Robert (not his real name) was a media type, a city slicker who'd been a self-described leftist. In his years in the media, he'd run around with powerful politicians, and he knew many of the movers and shakers on the Left. Legislated gay marriage, legalized abortion, the environmental movement, stripping God from the public square—he was all for it. But somehow he'd found himself at a conservative political rally, and I was the featured speaker.

The letter recounted how I'd stepped onto the stage in my signature outfit—camo pants and a flannel button-down—and I'd shared the good news of King Jesus. He'd come from heaven to earth with a particular intention, I said. Salvation of the souls of men. It was a statement Robert had never heard before, and as he listened, he was moved by the most shocking statement. It was so shocking, in fact, that he wrote it down.

"Mankind could not get our hands on God to harm him unless he became a human. So that's what God did. Ultimately, he was murdered by mankind, rose again, and that's how he saved the world."

Robert wrote about how he began shaking all over when he heard these words, how he was crushed by the realization that if God came into the world today, Robert would be among the crucifiers. It was the moment he knew he had to learn more about this God, this King of the universe who subjected himself to the lawless acts of men so he could save the world. He left the rally that night and began studying. He subscribed to BlazeTV so he could watch every episode of *In the Woods*, which is where he heard me say I'd never led a left-winger to Jesus. He started reading the Bible verses I cited in the show, which led him to other verses, other passages about King Jesus. And as he read, he believed.

His letter concluded by asking if he could visit Miss Kay and me on the river, and he left me his contact information. After I read the final sentence, I handed it to my redneck butler, Dan, and asked him to get in touch with Robert. "Invite that dude down to the river," and Dan promised he would.

A few weeks later, Robert sat in my living room and retold his story. He recounted his convictions, how he'd previously believed we should keep God out of government, how he supported using the law to advance godless policies. But when he heard of a God who had become human, he'd had a near out-of-body experience. It'd been the moment everything changed for him, and he knew he had to follow this King, whatever that meant. That decision had led him on a journey, and that journey had landed him on my couch.

We spent three hours together, talking through the truth of the gospel. And when our conversation drew to a close, I asked, "You been baptized yet?"

"Not yet," he said.

"You want to?"

"Let's do it."

And with that, Robert followed me out the front door and down to the receding waters of the Ouachita River. We slogged through the muddy silt the floodwaters had deposited, waded almost up to our knees before we made it to the river water. We went a little farther, and I asked him whether it was his intent to follow the law of the King, the law of love, for the rest of his life. He said it was. So I baptized him right there in the river in the name of the Father, Son, and the Holy Spirit.

Robert came out of the water a new man that day. He changed his clothes, ate a bite, then drove away from the Robertson camp happy, happy, happy. I've kept up with his progress. He's been true to his word and the Word of the Almighty. He's left the lawless ways of living behind and has signed on with the King. He's sharing his new life with the world around him (I hope he's shared extra with his liberal cronies), and as he has, the kingdom—the kingdom whose law is love—keeps moving forward.

WHAT IS THE LAW OF THE KINGDOM?

America was a country founded on the rule of law. And what was the foundation of that law? In both this book and in *The Theft of America's Soul*, I've gone to great lengths to show how our Founding Fathers created a system of laws based on God's Word. It was a system framed by the Constitution, and it was meant to protect religious liberty, promote personal responsibility, support American families, protect the innocent, value integrity and morality, and guard against the tyranny of monarchies. It was a legal system with checks and balances, one in which the United States Supreme Court was meant to ensure that every law in this country lined up with the Constitution framed by our Founders.

America's legal system started out on the right foot. Based in God's Word, with a legislature that began the day with prayer and subject to a court whose building had a depiction of Moses and the Ten Commandments on it, it seemed we were on the right track. And though we didn't get it perfect, though we still had profoundly ungodly policies and laws, such as slavery, we were still pointed in a God-honoring direction. (This is why Christian abolitionists were able to make political headway to outlaw slavery in the nineteenth century.) But Americans are no different than other humans on Planet Earth, and over the decades, we've lost sight of our godly heritage. Like every other people who've ever existed, we're so prone to wander.

Lord, I feel it.

I've seen that wandering over the course of my life, a wandering that gets worse as the years roll by. And if we'd wake up long enough to notice, we'd find we're wandering toward the edge of a very high cliff. And if world history is any indication, I suspect we'll eventually wander over the edge of that cliff just as other countries have, even to our ruin. After all, there's only one kingdom that stands forever, and it's certainly not America.

Earthly kingdoms come and go, and with them, their systems of law. The Scriptures say as much. In fact, in the Old Testament, the Almighty spoke to Nebuchadnezzar—the king of the known world six hundred years before Christ's birth—in a dream. Unable to interpret the dream, the king called Daniel, a young Jewish man living under the king's rule, and asked for the meaning. Unashamed and unafraid, Daniel recounted the dream in this way:

> Your Majesty looked, and there before you stood a large statue—an enormous, dazzling statue, awesome in appearance. The head of the statue was made of pure gold, its chest and arms of silver, its belly and thighs of bronze, its legs of iron, its feet partly of iron and partly of baked clay. While you were watching, a rock was cut out, but not by human hands. It struck the statue on its feet of iron and clay and smashed them. Then the iron, the clay, the bronze, the silver and the gold were all broken to pieces and became like chaff on a threshing floor in the summer. The wind swept them away without leaving a trace. But the rock that struck the statue became a huge mountain and filled the whole earth. (Dan. 2:31–35)

As for the interpretation, Daniel didn't pull any punches with old Nebuchadnezzar. He shared how the kingdom of Babylon, which was represented by the golden head, would be short-lived. The kingdom and its code would eventually give way to an inferior silver kingdom, a kingdom many Bible scholars believe to be the Persian Empire. The silver kingdom wouldn't stand forever either, and it'd fall to the bronze kingdom, which many interpret to be the Greek Empire. That bronze kingdom would give way to an iron kingdom, which would ultimately become a divided kingdom. (Sounds like the divided Roman Empire in the days of Jesus if you ask me.) And in the days of that divided empire, the true kingdom, the eternal kingdom would come. Daniel put it this way:

> In the time of those kings, the God of heaven will set up a kingdom that will never be destroyed, nor will it be left to another people. It will crush all those kingdoms and bring them to an end, but it will itself endure forever. This is the meaning of the vision of the rock cut out of a mountain, but not by human hands—a rock that broke the iron, the bronze, the clay, the silver and the gold to pieces. (vv. 44–45)

The most famous kingdoms of the earth, with all their man-made government structures and legal codes, would be crushed by the rock, the eternal kingdom. What is that rock? Consider Jesus' words after Peter rightly identified Jesus as the Messiah, the awaited king of Israel. Jesus said, "On this rock, I will build my church, and the gates [or the kingdom] of Hades will not overcome it" (Matt. 16:18).

Jesus was clear about his kingship, and he was clear on the

laws ordering his kingdom. In fact, he shared the two greatest laws in all the kingdom: love God with everything you have and love your neighbors as yourself (Matt. 22:37–39). He taught that his kingdom was not marked by the politics of power. Instead, he said:

> The kings of the Gentiles lord it over them; and those who exercise authority over them call themselves Benefactors. But you are not to be like that. Instead, the greatest among you should be like the youngest, and the one who rules like the one who serves. For who is greater, the one who is at the table or the one who serves? Is it not the one who is at the table? But I am among you as one who serves. (Luke 22:25–27)

The gospel of John records Jesus' revolutionary law this way: "A new command [or law] I give you: Love one another. As I have loved you, so you must love one another. By this everyone will know that you are my disciples, if you love one another" (13:34–35).

In the eternal kingdom, there was a certain kind of law and order. It was not the law and order that came through passing law after law, through regulating every human behavior. Instead, order in the kingdom comes through practicing love and service. But this begs the question, how exactly did Jesus love and serve others?

Jesus healed the lame and lepers, there's no doubt about that. He provided food for the hungry and even a little wine for a wedding where the well had run dry. He met people where they had physical needs, but he never shied away from sharing hard spiritual truths. He called the people to repent by saying, "The kingdom of heaven has come near" (Matt. 4:17). He instructed the woman caught in adultery to "go now and leave your life of sin" (John 8:11). He called the rich to leave their luxuries, the sinners and tax collectors to leave behind their sinful ways, and the religious leaders to leave all their hollow laws. He warned them all: "Unless you repent, you too will all perish" (Luke 13:3).

You see, the law of love provides for both our physical and spiritual needs. It warns of sinful living and godless laws. It calls people to repentance and asks them to live in the kingdom of love. So ask yourself: *Do I put my trust in the laws of men or do I live out the kingdom law of love, the law that serves others and invites them to repent?* Put another way, I might ask: *Do you put your trust in American politics or Jesus Politics?*

WE CARRY THE LAW OF LOVE

The kingdom of God has come, and we are ambassadors of the King. We are subject to its law, the law of love, and that law is higher than any bill passed by the legislators in Washington or any other state of the Union. The law of the kingdom of God is outside the jurisdiction of the United States Supreme Court too.

Practically speaking, what does this mean for those who want to follow King Jesus?

- When the Supreme Court affirms laws allowing abortion on demand, the people of the kingdom should resist, demonstrating love toward the unborn baby and his or her mother.
- When any legislative body changes the definition of marriage, the people of the kingdom should call their politicians,

judges, and neighbors to repent and to love, honor, and cherish their spouse of the opposite sex all the way to death.

- When any arm of the government tries to cram some god-less, unconstitutional law into our lives, the citizens of the kingdom should respond in love, calling our country to repent.

As you're repenting, also begin serving the King by serving others and calling your neighbors to repent. You'll be able to watch as they find new freedom. Freedom from lust and runaway sexual desire? Sure, because all our desires will be met in the spouses we love, the spouses the King has given us. Freedom from anger, hate, and violence? You bet, because the love of the King will cast out all violence. Freedom from the chains of death that plague us all? That's the best part of living by the law of love.

And for a moment just imagine a world changed by the law of love practiced among the people. Wouldn't our country be so much different? Our abortion rates, divorce rates, suicide rates, murder rates, sexually transmitted disease rates—wouldn't they drop to something near zero? Would we spend so much of our time debating healthcare if we provided for our sick neighbors like we provide for ourselves, if the big pharmaceutical companies were run by people who loved the King? Would we continue to hear of mass shootings in the news? Nah. How do I know? Just ask yourself: *When's the last time a godly person, a Jesus-loving Christian who lives by the Bible, shot up a school?*

When we live by the law of the King, the law of love, we bring natural order to our lives. And if enough of us did that, if enough of us traded our political ideologies for Jesus Politics, just as Robert did, the face of America would change.

THERE'S ONLY ONE LAW THAT
CAN SAVE AMERICA

Make no mistake, America is an earthly kingdom just like any other, and all earthly kingdoms fall. But if we return to the principles of the King, if we do our best to embody the law of love, we might be able to stave off total collapse for a while. Maybe even a few generations. But even if we can't keep America from being crushed to dust like every other kingdom on earth, we can live for a kingdom that's more eternal, one that never ends. And we can invite others into it.

So as you consider how to apply the law of love required by Jesus Politics, ask yourself:

- Which politicians answer to the higher law, the law of love?
- Which policies advance the law of the King, the law of love?
- Even if America continues its downward spiral of hate and death, how can you continue to spread the love of God through calling our country to repentance?

Answer these questions as best you can. Then go out there and act in accordance with that higher law. Fight against immoral laws. Help your neighbor. Call the people around you to repentance. And everywhere you go, work to advance the kingdom that crushes all other kingdoms.

A KINGDOM MANIFESTO

THE PROBLEM:
America, whose legal foundations were laid
on biblical principles, has enacted ungodly,
unbiblical laws that lead to death.

THE MANIFESTO OF THE KING:
The law of the kingdom is higher than any
law passed by men; it is the law of love.

A MANIFESTO IN ACTION:
Speak out against ungodly laws and serve
your fellow man. Call people to repent and
join the King whose law is always love.

CHAPTER 11

Changing America Through Kingdom Living

There we were in New York City, getting the word out about *In the Woods with Phil*, *The Theft of America's Soul*, and *Unashamed*. After leaving the Trump International Hotel, we'd hit the ground running, which seems to be what everyone in New York City does. Show after show, we made the rounds. And one of those rounds was to *Varney & Co.* on Fox Business. My message was clear and unashamed. And as old Stuart Varney found out, I came fully loaded with a double-barrel helping of the Almighty's truth.

I opened the interview the way I opened every time. I shared how all have fallen short of the glory of God, all are living under the law of sin, and all would die. I shared how every human on Planet Earth needed the saving work of Jesus and how it was my hope to share that truth with as many people as I could.

"The resurrection of the dead," I said, "that's the message we proclaim whether to kings, monarchs, presidents, or talk-show hosts."

Varney laughed. "A talk-show host? Is that what I am now?" Brushing off my accidental sleight, he turned to Jase.

"Jase, you just don't hear that proclamation of faith, that Christian faith. . . . You don't hear it. I mean, television these days, especially television news, is secular. Do you want to change that?"

"Yeah," Jase said, and then he went on to share how our goal wasn't so much to change television as it was to lead people into the kingdom, regardless of the position they held. This included the Trump family, and he shared how our family had come into contact with theirs by way of the close encounter with hotel security. Then Jase dropped a bomb on Varney. Speaking about the Trump camp, he said, "They reached out to me, and we started having spiritual discussions because that's what we're all about."

"You've had spiritual discussions with the president of the United States?" Varney asked wide-eyed.

"I have with his son," Jase said. "And my dad has with President Trump. And here's the deal: They're open."

I jumped in, explained how the president was a work in progress as far as following Jesus was concerned. Still, the president had done more good for Christianity than any president in my lifetime, at least as far as I was concerned. And though I didn't run down the list of his religious bona fides, I replayed some of his greatest hits in my mind. He defunded Planned Parenthood to the tune of millions of dollars. He invited Christian leaders to pray for him in the Oval Office on more than one occasion. He appointed an outspoken Christian as the US ambassador at large for international religious freedom, Senator Sam Brownback, who hosted an event to advance religious freedom.

At the end of the interview, I closed with the simplest message, a message that might change America if we'd let it. "Love God, love each other. It's the message of the Bible," I said. "For the life of me, I don't see the downside. What about you, Varney?"

I shared the truth with Mr. Varney just like I had with so many I come into contact with, whether paupers or presidents. I was clear. Unashamed. And interview after interview that day, I continued to do the same thing. I shared the message of the kingdom with Neil Cavuto on his show. I shared it with Sean Hannity too. In fact, Jase took it a step further with Mr. Hannity, offering to baptize him in an alligator-infested bayou. (I assured Mr. Hannity, "It's not the alligators you have to worry about. It's the cottonmouths that will get you.")

After a couple of days of publicity appearances, we made our way back to northern Louisiana. There, I got back to my morning routine: setting out the crawfish traps, tending to the fields, sitting in the woods and watching the morning roll by. As I did, I considered that weeklong trip, how it'd been a success as far as I was concerned. But whether we gained new listeners or readers, it didn't much matter to me. We'd gone to New York for one reason: to share the good news of Jesus and to invite people to turn to the Almighty and live good and godly lives. We shared how if enough people lived these kinds of good and godly kingdom lives, they might change America if we'd let it. And as far as I could tell, millions had heard that message.

SHARE YOUR FAITH, DO GOOD,
AND CHANGE LIVES

I do my best to carry my faith everywhere I go. As far as I can tell, so do my boys and their families. The Robertson camp lives their faith out loud in the public sector. We preach it on television shows, podcasts, and in books. But we don't just share it when the cameras are rolling. We live it out in our day-to-day lives too.

- We read the Word of God every day and attend Bible studies because we're followers of the King.
- We pray with family and friends because we're followers of the King.
- We share our faith with anyone who crosses our path because we're followers of the King.
- We get up early, work hard, and don't complain because we're followers of the King.
- We honor our parents, our wives, and our neighbors because we're followers of the King.
- We help women who're on their way to the abortion clinics because we're followers of the King.
- We share our bounty, our catfish, our crawfish, and our money with our neighbors because we're followers of the King.
- We speak to those in our community about godless socialism, religious liberty, marriage, and the family because we're followers of the King.
- We have conversations with politicians and media

personalities that never make the news. Why? You guessed it. Because we're followers of the one and only eternal King.

It's like I said to Mr. Varney. We're out to change America one life at a time. How do we do that? We share the love of Jesus in word *and* in deed. We strive "to do what is good for each other and for everyone else" (1 Thess. 5:15). And what does it mean to do good? It means doing just as Jesus would. And this is what I call *kingdom living.*

In the book of Acts, Peter met with a group of Gentiles who were previously considered outsiders to the kingdom of God. Convinced by God that these people were to become followers of King Jesus, Peter shared the good news of his life with them:

> You know what has happened throughout the province of Judea, beginning in Galilee after the baptism that John preached— how God anointed Jesus of Nazareth with the Holy Spirit and power, and how he went around doing good and healing all who were under the power of the devil, because God was with him. (10:37–38)

King Jesus came preaching the truth, but he also fed the people, healed diseases, raised the dead, and set free those who were trapped in religious shackles. The agenda of the King was to do good everywhere he went and, through it, to break the evil one's hold on people's hearts and to invite them into a new way of living, namely, kingdom living.

Teach, preach, and do good. This could have been the kingdom-living slogan of the early church. It wasn't just Peter who used it either. In his letter to the young preacher Titus, Paul encouraged various groups within the church to do good:

- Each elder was to "be blameless—not overbearing, not quick-tempered, not given to drunkenness, not violent, not pursuing dishonest gain. Rather he must be hospitable, one who loves what is *good*, who is self-controlled, upright, holy and disciplined" (Titus 1:7–8).
- Older women were "to be reverent in the way they lived, not to be slanderers or addicted to much wine, but to *teach what is good*" (2:3).
- Titus was to set an example for the young men of the church "by *doing what is good*" (2:7).
- The entire church was to be "eager to *do what is good*" (2:14).
- Titus was to "remind the people to be subject to the rulers and authorities, to be obedient, to be ready to *do whatever is good*" (3:1).
- Those who trusted in God were to "be careful to devote themselves to *doing what is good*" (3:8).
- Paul closed the letter: "Our people must learn to devote themselves to *doing what is good*, in order to provide for urgent needs and not live unproductive lives" (3:14).

In one of the shortest books of the Bible, weighing in at only three chapters, Paul asked the people to do and teach good no less than seven times. As far as he was concerned, followers of the King were to be outspoken and live action-oriented lives, lives worthy of the King. But how did he describe those who didn't live lives worthy of the King? In the opening of his letter, he wrote:

"They claim to know God, but by their actions they deny him. They are detestable, disobedient and unfit for doing anything good" (1:16). And in the book of Romans he wrote a similar sentiment: "To those who by persistence in doing good seek glory, honor and immortality, he will give eternal life. But for those who are self-seeking and who reject the truth and follow evil, there will be wrath and anger" (2:7–8).

It ain't rocket science, America. In fact, it's so simple it might be called *redneck* science. If we follow God in teaching, preaching, and doing good, we'll be blessed. If we don't? If we turn our backs on God's good and follow our own desires, we'll reap an ungodly harvest of murder, death, and destruction. (You wonder why there are so many school shootings these days?)

So as you consider the platform positions of the world versus those of Jesus Politics, ask yourself which sounds like doing good:

- The government's interference with our right to worship the Almighty *or* allowing people to practice their faith in the public sector?
- Taking away a democratic people's ability to fight against tyranny without addressing the hate in the human heart *or* standing up for the rights established by our Founding Fathers?
- Elevating the creation over the Creator *or* worshipping the Creator before creation?
- Terminating human life *or* saving human life?
- Is it good to deprive a child of both a mother and father *or* is it better to protect God's definition of marriage?
- Is asking the government to provide high-cost, unsustainable,

temporary healthcare good *or* is it better to seek eternal healthcare and then chip in to provide for the needs of your neighbor?

I could go on and on, but the idea of preaching, teaching, and doing good goes well beyond the platform issues of Jesus Politics. It involves practical things, too, like serving our neighbors, inviting them over to share a pot of beans, a pan of cornbread, or a mess of crawfish harvested from the river. Doing good might mean creating jobs for our unemployed neighbors or giving them interest-free loans for a medical need. It means sharing the good news of Jesus with them, and when they move on it, inviting them into the waters of baptism.

Doing good means loving our neighbors. That's what the King did, and imitating him is the way to go.

WHEN DOING GOOD MEANS REVOLUTION

As I wrote in *Theft*, it seems America has bought into the lies of the evil one, seems like we're on a slow slide away from the good toward godlessness, and our politicians are leading the charge. Some promote an atheistic socialist agenda. Some undermine the family, call marriage between the same sex normal. They've legalized child killing, nature worshipping, some forms of drug abuse, and debauchery. They are "lovers of themselves, lovers of money, boastful, proud, abusive, disobedient to their parents, ungrateful, unholy, without love, unforgiving, slanderous, without self-control, brutal, not lovers of the good, treacherous, rash, conceited, lovers of pleasure rather than lovers of God"

(2 Tim. 3:2–4). They've set the conditions for godless tyranny, and they've smiled while doing it.

And as the politicians (and their backers in Hollywood and New York City) continue to push a godless agenda, as they continue to advance a creeping tyranny that seeks to silence the voices of believers, followers of the Almighty ought to be aware. We ought to be prayerful, understanding that a day might come when doing good and loving our neighbors might mean standing up for our beliefs.

What do I mean?

I believe that sometimes doing good requires a more prophetic approach. And so I've taken my message to the streets, spoken out against the culture of sin advanced by Washington and New York and Hollywood. And if it came down to it, if the government required me to follow ungodly laws, I'd have to put my money where my mouth is. I'd have to choose doing what's godly over obeying those laws. Would I be justified in disobeying ungodly laws? Thomas Jefferson thought so.

Jefferson, Founding Father and drafter of the Declaration of Independence, knew there were certain God-given rights that no government should trample. In the Declaration, he wrote the words you probably know by heart: "We hold these truths to be self-evident, that all men are created equal, that they are endowed by their Creator with certain unalienable Rights, that among these are Life, Liberty, and the pursuit of Happiness." In that same Declaration of Independence, he went on to write these words, words that many do not know by heart:

> That whenever any Form of Government becomes destructive
> to these ends, it is the Right of the People to alter or to abol-
> ish it, and to institute new Government, laying its foundation

on such principles and organizing its powers in such form, as to them shall seem most likely to affect their Safety and Happiness. . . . But when a long train of abuses and usurpations, pursuing invariably the same Object evinces a design to reduce them under absolute Despotism, it is their right, it is their duty, to throw off such Government, and to provide new Guards for their future security.[1]

Jefferson followed this statement with a series of twenty-seven grievances against the tyranny of King George III, grievances which were getting in the way of his subjects' God-given rights. And after declaring independence from King George, Jefferson and his crew fought to establish a country that protected and promoted the rights given by one true King: King Jesus.

Our Founding Fathers showed us the truth. Sometimes doing good means challenging unjust and ungodly laws. But we don't simply get our authority to challenging ungodly laws from the Founding Fathers. King Jesus himself showed how true kingdom living sometimes involves some form of action.

Jesus, the man who did good in every way, refused to follow the unjust and ungodly laws and rules of his own society from time to time. In his day, a group of religious lawyers brought a woman to him who'd been caught in adultery, the legal penalty for which was public execution by stoning. Did Jesus uphold the unjust law and terminate the woman's life? Nope. Instead, he showed mercy, turning the law around on those trying to enforce it. To the men holding rocks, he said, "Let any one of you who is without sin be the first to throw a stone at her" (John 8:7). The men, of course, turned tail and walked away.

Sometimes words were not enough, though. Just before his unjust crucifixion, Jesus entered Jerusalem to celebrate the Passover. There he saw the moneychangers in the temple swindling the people by selling impure animals, a practice that was perfectly legal. He turned the tables over and drove the merchants out, telling them not to dirty the house of the Almighty (Mark 11:15–17). He rebelled against the order of the day, likely breaking a law or two in the process. And why? Because he believed protecting the house of the King was more important than going along with the immoral, godless, swindling behavior of the religious leaders of the day.

Consider the stories listed in this book. Remember Jack Phillips who refused to bake a cake for a same-sex couple although the laws of his community labeled his refusal as hate speech? Remember the folks at Hobby Lobby and how they refused to provide health insurance coverage for abortion services? And outside of those stories, consider the thousands of Bible-believing pastors in America who may one day have to choose between honoring God's definition of the family or performing same-sex weddings. Consider a day when speaking out about Christian beliefs might be labeled a federal offense.

Yes, kingdom living requires us to do good so long as we have the freedom to pursue it. But it requires us to stand firm in our faith, too, even if it means being mocked by the media, having our businesses shut down, or even being imprisoned. It means fighting for the right to live a godly life and never capitulating to the evil one.

So as you consider what it means to live a kingdom-oriented life, as you consider how to advance what's godly and how to fight against what's evil, particularly in the realm of Jesus Politics, ask yourself these questions:

- Do I strive to live a good and godly life? Do I take my kingdom living to the streets?
- Do I speak out and act against unjust or ungodly laws, laws that would require me to disobey the King?
- Which political candidate does their best to do good according to the Word of God, even if they're only a work in progress? Will they fight to preserve those rights endowed to me by my creator, the Almighty?
- Which politicians will appoint judges who will strike down laws that keep Christians from living out their kingdom principles?
- Should everything melt down, which politicians will do what it takes to fight for, establish, and protect those of us who do our best to pursue the kingdom?

Ask these questions as you wrestle with the issues during this political season. And keep this list handy for the political seasons to come. If I had my guess, it's a list of questions that will only become more important with every passing election cycle. But more than asking these questions and casting your vote, do your part for the kingdom by doing good, by living godly lives that influence the world around you. Invite folks to your table, share your resources, speak out against godless tyranny, then share the good news of King Jesus with everyone. Who knows, maybe one or two will join you in this journey of kingdom living. And if enough of us bring just one or two new people into this way of Jesus Politics, we might become a political force to be reckoned with. We might become a mighty throng ready to win back the soul of America.

— A KINGDOM MANIFESTO —

THE PROBLEM:
America has turned its back on the Almighty
and, as a result, is faltering in doing good.

THE MANIFESTO OF THE KING:
Live a life worthy of the King by doing
good, teaching good, and speaking out
against the things that are not good.

A MANIFESTO IN ACTION:
Live your lives in a manner worthy of the King,
in a way that invites others into the kingdom in
the hope of winning back the soul of America.

CHAPTER 12

Taking the Manifesto to the Street

Miss Kay and I are what some might call community activists, although we just call ourselves followers of the King. We work with the down and out, the drunks, the drug addicts, and those mired in sexual sin, regardless of color, creed, or sexual orientation. We deal with the people most Americans wouldn't give the time of day to. We welcome folks who carry everything they own in a backpack or, if they're really well off, an old clunker of a car. We welcome the wealthy too. And in our neck of the woods, we've gained a reputation for it. (It bears mentioning that many others in our local community have the same reputation for kingdom living.)

Among those folks who've made their way down to the river was a young, evidently struggling woman who looked like she hadn't eaten in weeks. Bone thin, hair almost as wild as my beard, she walked into our church a few years ago and sat in front of me and Miss Kay for an entire service. After the closing hymn and prayer, she turned to me and said, "Mr. Robertson, could you help me?"

I took one look at her. Strung out. Helpless. Probably not a dime to her name. I was moved with compassion.

"Sure," I said. "Let's gather a few of my friends and talk it out." And that's exactly what we did.

To a circle of my most trusted friends, she explained how she'd had just enough for a bus ticket from Arizona, how she wanted to make her way to the Robertson family because she'd seen *Duck Dynasty* and thought maybe we could give her some answers. She shared about her heroin use, how the drug had its hooks in her, and how she needed a way out. Could we help?

Sure we could, I told her. But she'd need to do a few things. She'd need a rehab bed for a few weeks, and then she'd need a place to land when she got out. She'd need to find a job and hold it down, something that could instill her with a little dignity. More than any of that, though, she'd need a faith to hold onto. She'd need the stability that only a King can bring.

She listened and followed the advice my friends and I gave her. She cleaned up, got a job, and became a child of the King. Miss Kay put her up in a rental house. We found her a beat-up but serviceable vehicle. She worked the plan and found so much freedom.

Freedom from drugs? Yes.

Freedom from welfare and government assistance? Yes.

Freedom from sin and death and ultimately the grave? You bet.

Sometime after her recovery, she sent a note to me through Miss Kay. It was a simple note of gratitude: "Mr. Robertson, thank you for giving me hope."

Hope for the hopeless. That's what happens when followers

of the King carry his message to the world without reservation. That's what happens when we're unashamed of the good news of Jesus.

Jesus Politics is about more than changing government structures and systems. Jesus Politics is about loving the King so much that you'd go out of your way to share that love with your neighbors. King Jesus himself said this is what life is all about. He taught, "'Love the Lord your God with all your heart and with all your soul and with all your mind.' This is the first and greatest commandment. And the second is like it: 'Love your neighbor as yourself'" (Matt. 22:37–39).

If we truly love our neighbors, won't we share the way of the King with them? And if we love America, won't we do whatever we can to preserve our freedoms to share that love?

No matter where I go, no matter what I do, I keep my eyes and ears tuned to the loving work of the King. Sometimes that work takes me to a place where I address political issues, where I do my part to speak out about abortion or religious liberty or the Second Amendment or healthcare or whatever. Sometimes it takes me to the grass roots though, to those who need help getting off drugs, off the welfare roll, and off the hit list of the evil one. And when those opportunities come up, I move on them. In love. Why? Because I'm a servant of the King, called to live out my life just as he would.

So as this discussion of Jesus Politics draws to its conclusion, remember this: Jesus Politics is not about supporting a particular political agenda. Jesus Politics isn't just meant to give you debate points or talking points for those social media sites everyone seems to love these days. It's not even just about what you do in the voting booth. Ultimately, Jesus Politics is about loving

God, loving our neighbors, and doing whatever it takes to bring, maintain, and protect his kingdom on earth as it is in heaven.

THE TRUE KING WILL HAVE THE LAST LAUGH

How have I seen our country change in these seventy-three years I've been alive? A good question, I guess. I can remember a day and age when our parents taught us to love God, obey authority, and show respect for the men and women who served this country. We may not have always agreed with the president, but we showed him respect and honor. We pledged allegiance to the flag before school, said a prayer for our country. We did our best to help our neighbors, too, particularly since the federal government wasn't making grand promises of free healthcare or housing or whatever. The country seemed less divided, less fragile. We the People were a family.

Times have changed, though, and if you ask me, it's not been for the best. We've thrown God out of the public arena, legalized abortion, and changed the definition of marriage. We've adopted policies that advance a socialist agenda, policies like free healthcare for all. We worship nature instead of the Creator of that nature. We're on the brink of undoing the Second Amendment. We follow every sexual desire we have. We've seen the disintegration of the home, higher rates of drug addiction and homelessness, and a complete breakdown of the fabric of America. How might I sum it up? Chaos. Lawlessness. Sin runs wild. If I had to describe it in biblical terms, I might call it the end of days.

We're a couple of millennia removed from the writing of the

New Testament, but it seems more applicable today than ever. In fact, it seems to describe the present culture of America. Consider Paul's second letter to Timothy, in which he gave the citizens of the kingdom instructions for living in a godless age:

> Flee the evil desires of youth and pursue righteousness, faith, love and peace, along with those who call on the Lord out of a pure heart. Don't have anything to do with foolish and stupid arguments, because you know they produce quarrels. And the Lord's servant must not be quarrelsome but must be kind to everyone, able to teach, not resentful. Opponents must be gently instructed, in the hope that God will grant them repentance leading them to a knowledge of the truth, and that they will come to their senses and escape from the trap of the devil, who has taken them captive to do his will. (2:22–26)

See there? Followers of the King were to chase after the King. Pursue the King. They were to love their neighbors and be kind to them. But they were also to gently instruct and warn the leaders of the world of the schemes of the evil one. They were to take the manifesto of the King to the streets in an effort to save the people from surefire destruction.

Destruction?

Yes, destruction, America. Pay attention to Paul's prophecy:

> But mark this: There will be terrible times in the last days. People will be lovers of themselves, lovers of money, boastful, proud, abusive, disobedient to their parents, ungrateful, unholy, without love, unforgiving, slanderous, without self-control, brutal, not lovers of the good, treacherous, rash, conceited, lovers of

161

pleasure rather than lovers of God—having a form of godliness but denying its power. Have nothing to do with such people.

They are the kind who worm their way into homes and gain control over gullible women, who are loaded down with sins and are swayed by all kinds of evil desires, always learning but never able to come to a knowledge of the truth. . . . They are men of depraved minds, who, as far as the faith is concerned, are rejected. (2 Tim. 3:1–8)

Sound familiar? Start down the list Paul wrote out and ask yourself: *Does that list describe our current political candidates? Are they lovers of themselves, lovers of money, boastful, proud, and sometimes abusive? Are they unholy, unforgiving, slanderous, without self-control, or lovers of good? Are they treacherous, rash, conceited? Do they love pleasure and power more than the Almighty? Do they genuinely love their neighbors?* (Which begs the question, When's the last time you heard a politician say I love you?) And what did Paul say about the end of these sorts of people? In his letter to the Philippians, he wrote: "For, as I have often told you before and now tell you again even with tears, many live as enemies of the cross of Christ. Their destiny is destruction" (3:18–19).

If I'm honest, I'd say the current political landscape in America looks a lot like the last days Paul described, the days that will inevitably lead to destruction. In fact, it's uncanny. Maybe even surreal. But here's the truth that should bring us great comfort, and it comes right out of the Scriptures:

Why do the nations conspire
and the peoples plot in vain?

The kings of the earth rise up
and the rulers band together
against the LORD and against his anointed, saying,
"Let us break their chains
and throw off their shackles."
The One enthroned in heaven laughs;
the Lord scoffs at them.
He rebukes them in his anger
and terrifies them in his wrath, saying,
"I have installed my king
on Zion, my holy mountain." (Psalm 2:1–6)

Yes, American politicians can do all their plotting and scheming. They can pretend they're in control, that they know better than the Almighty, that they can somehow free us from his rules for living, maybe lead us into a more progressive, scientific, utopian future. They can change the laws to suit their desires and chase the sin of the day. They can try to kill God, ignore him, or deny his kingdom, but no matter how hard they try, they cannot stand against the one true King: King Jesus. And when the final day comes, when King Jesus returns, I want to be found worthy. I want to be found carrying his standard. Loving people the way he would. Letting my faith lead my time, talent, resources, and my vote. I want to be found at his side, laughing alongside him at the hollow schemes of men.

SO WHAT CAN YOU DO?

If we don't change course, America is headed toward chaos and destruction. If we keep chasing our desires and entitlements, if we keep passing laws that call evil good and good evil, we'll find ourselves wrapping up this constitutional experiment, sure enough. But no matter which course the American political system takes, those who turn their eyes to the King and trust in his saving power will be spared from the surefire destruction that's coming.

Yes, we know destruction is coming, and even if it's not in this decade, humankind can't escape it forever. The writer of the letter to the Hebrews assures us that even in the face of that destruction, there is a way of escape. Who delivered the message about that way of escape? Jesus. And pay attention to how the author described him:

> In the past God spoke to our ancestors through the prophets at many times and in various ways, but in these last days he has spoken to us by his Son, whom he appointed heir of all things, and through whom also he made the universe. The Son is the radiance of God's glory and the exact representation of his being, sustaining all things by his powerful word. After he had provided purification for sins, he sat down at the right hand of the Majesty in heaven. So he became as much superior to the angels as the name he has inherited is superior to theirs. (1:1–4)

As if to make himself even more clear, the writer continued:

> But about his Son he says, "Your throne . . . will last for ever and ever; a scepter of justice will be the scepter of your kingdom." (v. 8)

Jesus, the heir of all things, the radiance of God's glory, the one who sits on the throne and holds the scepter of justice over his kingdom is the King who provided a way of escape. And that being the case, the author of Hebrew instructed us:

> We must pay the most careful attention, therefore, to what we have heard, so that we do not drift away. For since the message spoken through angels was binding, and every violation and disobedience received its just punishment, how shall we escape if we ignore so great a salvation? This salvation, which was first announced by the Lord, was confirmed to us by those who heard him. God also testified to it by signs, wonders and various miracles, and by gifts of the Holy Spirit distributed according to his will. (2:1–4)

The sad truth is that America hasn't paid careful attention to the truth we once knew. We've drifted away. Like the Romans, the French, and our brothers and sisters in the United Kingdom, we've strayed from the truth we once held so dear. But even if our country continues on its slow slide to disobedience and punishment, even if we continue toward destruction at breakneck speed, there's good news for the followers of the King. We can be saved, even if our democracy, our country, or even our environment burns to the ground. Yes, the world might grind to a halt, but our salvation is secure if we follow the King. I know, because the Bible says as much.

The prophet Isaiah assured us that the whole world (which includes its political systems) is on the way to winding down. He wrote:

> All the stars in the sky will be dissolved
> and the heavens rolled up like a scroll;

165

    all the starry hosts will fall

    like withered leaves from the vine,

    like shriveled figs from the fig tree. (34:4)

Still, the people were not to worry. Why? Because even though all the systems of the world perish, the King was on the scene, and he promised,

    My salvation will last forever,

    my righteousness will never fail. (Isa. 51:6)

The writers of the New Testament also knew that the nations, government systems, and even the world itself were headed toward the final judgment. In his first letter to the Corinthians, Paul wrote:

What I mean, brothers and sisters, is that the time is short. From now on those who have wives should live as if they did not; those who mourn, as if they did not; those who are happy, as if they were not; those who buy something, as if it were not theirs to keep; those who use the things of the world, as if not engrossed in them. For this world in its present form is passing away. (7:29–31)

But just because the world was passing away didn't mean there was no hope. The followers of the King were given a specific charge. Paul put it this way in his second letter to the same church: "We fix our eyes not on what is seen, but on what is unseen, since what is seen is temporary, but what is unseen is eternal" (2 Cor. 4:18).

Peter offered similar advice in his letter to the young churches across Asia Minor. He shared about the coming end of the age too. But he didn't stop there. He wrote about how the citizens of the King should live as that end approached:

> But the day of the Lord will come like a thief. The heavens will disappear with a roar; the elements will be destroyed by fire, and the earth and everything done in it will be laid bare.
>
> Since everything will be destroyed in this way, what kind of people ought you to be? You ought to live holy and godly lives as you look forward to the day of God and speed its coming. That day will bring about the destruction of the heavens by fire, and the elements will melt in the heat. But in keeping with his promise we are looking forward to a new heaven and a new earth, where righteousness dwells. (2 Peter 3:10–13)

And if this advice wasn't specific enough, he added:

> So then, dear friends, since you are looking forward to this, make every effort to be found spotless, blameless and at peace with him. Bear in mind that our Lord's patience means salvation, just as our dear brother Paul also wrote you with the wisdom God gave him. (vv. 14–15)

John also shared about the passing nature of the world as compared to the eternal promises of God: "The world and its desires pass away, but whoever does the will of God lives forever" (1 John 2:17).

So, America, as we continue down the path of degradation and destruction, I'll keep preaching the truth like some southern swamp prophet. I'll keep sharing with the hope that our country will turn away from sin and plot a course back to the Almighty, the King of kings. I'll vote in ways that protect our freedoms, our religious liberty, and that give us the best chance to return to the King. But even if our country doesn't correct its course, even if we continue on this slow slide to the coming destruction, I'll do my best to live a life that's godly, one that's blameless, spotless, and at peace with the King. I'll do my best to bring as many along as I can too.

I hope you'll make the same commitments. I hope you'll support candidates who follow the King and vote for policies in line with his causes. More than that, though, I hope you'll live out the King's mandates, whether you're a King-loving river rat from northern Louisiana, a King-loving rancher from Montana, or a King-loving city slicker from New York City. I hope you'll preach and teach the good news of the King wherever you go and live a life worthy of the coming salvation.

MY POLITICAL PARTY: THE PARTY OF THE KING

Wherever I go, I make my political affiliation clear: I ride with King Jesus. All the way to the end of the line. All the way into eternity. So when it comes to advancing the Jesus Politics manifesto in the political sector, don't play the partisan games of the day. Don't buy the lie that one side has it all together. Instead, pay attention to the individual politicians and their platforms. Ask yourself:

- Are they God-fearing?
- Do they give more than just lip service to the King?

- Do they protect religious liberty?
- Do they value and protect life?
- Will they support the traditional notions of the family and pass laws to strengthen this fundamental unit of American life?
- Will they protect our Second Amendment rights?
- Do they value the Creator over creation?
- Will they protect our right to earn money and to make a living in the ways God has called us to?
- Will they force us to accept unaffordable, less-desirable healthcare or will they point you to the only one who can save you from death and raise you from the grave?
- Will they advance the policies of the King?

Then make your political choice. But don't stop there. Take your Jesus Politics to the street. Ask yourself:

- Could my neighbor use a little help?
- Is there something I can do about the poverty in my city?
- Is there a convict I could visit, either one on parole or one in prison?
- Is there a woman who's considering abortion, one who'd keep her baby if she had better options?
- Am I friends with someone in a struggling marriage, someone I could encourage to commit their family to the King?
- How can I invite others away from their lives of sin and into the kingdom?

As you look for ways to take your renewed political affiliation to the grassroots, remember: Jesus Politics is about recognizing the work of Jesus all around you and about acting on that truth. Jesus Politics is about serving the King, protecting the King, and offering the love of the King to the world. As we do just that, we'll find ourselves walking into an eternal reward. How do I know? Jesus said as much:

> Then the King will say to those on his right, "Come, you who are blessed by my Father; take your inheritance, the kingdom prepared for you since the creation of the world. For I was hungry and you gave me something to eat, I was thirsty and you gave me something to drink, I was a stranger and you invited me in, I needed clothes and you clothed me, I was sick and you looked after me, I was in prison and you came to visit me."
>
> Then the righteous will answer him, "Lord, when did we see you hungry and feed you, or thirsty and give you something to drink? When did we see you a stranger and invite you in, or needing clothes and clothe you? When did we see you sick or in prison and go to visit you?"
>
> The King will reply, "Truly I tell you, whatever you did for one of the least of these brothers and sisters of mine, you did for me." (Matt. 25:34–40)

So go out there and do good on behalf of the King. Vote in ways consistent with Jesus Politics. Live good, morally pure lives, lives befitting the King. Do acts of service in love, showing the King's care for everyone you come into contact with. Be a worker in the fields of harvest, one who helps bring souls into the kingdom. Help build that mighty throng of kingdom-living, Jesus-following do-gooders.

Followers of the King, whether in northern Louisiana,

Southern California, or New York City, let's get out there and do our thing. Let's take our kingdom manifesto to the streets, showing the world the difference a bunch of King worshippers can make. If enough of us do, if we stay the course, the history books will tell of the era in which America was almost lost. Those same books will record how a small but mighty band of believers fought for what was right, took Jesus Politics to the streets, and won back the soul of America. And when our children, grandchildren, and great-grandchildren read those history books to their own children, they'll remember the manifesto of their ancestors, folks who might be called the Re-Founding Fathers and Mothers. They'll remember our battle cry, and they'll make it their own: All hail the King!

The Kingdom Manifesto in Action

- Vote for leaders who will protect capitalism, the system that best allows people to direct their money toward kingdom causes.
- Vote for leaders who will promote religious liberty, protect our rights to practice Christianity in every public square, and who live lives aligned with Jesus Politics.
- Vote for leaders who seek to preserve gun rights while offering kingdom-based solutions to the anger that's tearing this country apart.
- Vote for leaders who elevate the Creator over creation, who don't use environmental hype to create fear and procure power.
- Vote for leaders who advance the policies of life, the policies of the King and look for opportunities to serve women with unexpected or unwanted pregnancies with the truth from the King for their circumstances.
- Vote for leaders who cling to the biblical view of the family, who promote policies designed to strengthen families instead of destroy them. Then promote organizations that do the same.
- Vote for leaders who protect the medical system from

godless politicians. Get involved in your community to help provide for the medical needs of those around you.

- Demand that our leaders reflect the character of Jesus, that they extend forgiveness and pave the way for meaningful political debate instead of continual partisan bickering.
- Speak out against ungodly laws and serve your fellow man. Call people to repent and join the King whose law is always love.
- Live your lives in a manner worthy of the King, in a way that invites others into the kingdom in the hopes of winning back the soul of America.

NOTES

Chapter 1: A Kingdom Manifesto

1. V. I. Lenin, "The Attitude of the Workers' Party to Religion," *Proletary* 45, May 13 (26), 1909, https://www.marxists.org /archive/lenin/works/1909/may/13.htm.
2. Noah Webster, *Value of the Bible and Excellence of the Christian Religion: For the Use of Families and Schools* (New Haven, CT: Durrie & Peck, 1834), 175.
3. Noah Webster, *A Dictionary of the English Language*, s.v. "Manifesto," (New York: N & J White, 1832.).

Chapter 2: The Kingdom Foundation

1. Noah Webster to James Madison, October 16, 1829, Founders Early Access, Rotunda, University Press of Virginia, Charlottesville, https://rotunda.upress.virginia.edu /founders/default.xqy?keys=FOEA-print-02–02–02–1897.
2. George Washington, "Farewell Address," September 19, 1796, The Papers of George Washington, University of Virginia, Charlottesville, http://gwpapers.virginia.edu/documents_gw /farewell/transcript.html.

3. George Washington, "General Orders, 2 May 1778," National Archives Founders Online, https://founders .archives.gov/documents/Washington/03-15-02-0016.
4. John Adams to Thomas Jefferson, June 28, 1813, quoted by Michael Novak, "Meacham Nods," *National Review*, December 13, 2007, https://www.nationalreview.com/2007/12 /meacham-nods-michael-novak/.
5. See "John Adams Diary 1, 18 November 1755–29 August 1756," Adams Family Papers: An Electronic Archive, Massachusetts Historical Society, Boston, https://www.masshist.org /digitaladams/archive/.
6. George Washington, "General Orders, 2 May 1778," National Archives Founders Online, https://founders.archives.gov /documents/Washington/03-15-02-0016.
7. Bernard Christian Steiner, *One Hundred and Ten Years of Bible Society Work in Maryland, 1810–1920* (Baltimore: Maryland Bible Society, 1921), 14.
8. Caleb Parke, "Ohio School Scrubs 92-Year-Old Ten Commandments Plaque After Atheists Complain," Fox News, July 1, 2019, https://www.foxnews.com/us/ohio-school-atheist -complain-ten-commandments.
9. David G. Savage, "Colorado Cake Maker Asks Supreme Court to Provide a Religious Liberty Right to Refuse Gay Couple," *Los Angeles Times*, September 12, 2017, https://www.latimes .com/politics/la-na-pol-court-religion-gays-20170912-story.html.
10. David French, "The Next Big Religious Freedom Case Just Landed at SCOTUS," *National Review*, July 26, 2019, https://www.nationalreview.com/corner/the-next -big-religious-freedom-case-just-landed-at-scotus/.

Chapter 3: On the King's Capital

1. Megan Specia, "'A Dumb Decision': U.S. Said to Waste $28 Million on Afghan Army Camouflage," *New York Times*, June 21, 2017, https://www.nytimes.com/2017/06/21/world/asia /afghanistan-army-uniform-camouflage.html.
2. Katie Glueck, "Joe Biden Denounces Hyde Amendment,

Reversing His Position," *New York Times*, June 6, 2019, https://www.nytimes.com/2019/06/06/us/politics/joe-biden-hyde-amendment.html.

3. Jessica Semega et al., "Income and Poverty in the United States: 2018," U.S. Census Bureau, September 10, 2019, Report no. P60–266, https://www.census.gov/library/publications/2019/demo/p60–266.html.

4. Office of the Assistant Secretary for Planning and Evaluation, "ASPE Issue Brief: Drug Testing Welfare Recipients: Recent Proposals and Continuing Controversies," U.S. Department of Health and Human Services, October 2011, https://aspe.hhs.gov/basic-report/drug-testing-welfare-recipients-recent-proposals-and-continuing-controversies.

Chapter 4: On Gun Ownership in the Kingdom of Love

1. During the writing of this book, Bennet was a 2020 presidential hopeful.

2. Jason Gruenauer, "'It's About Kendrick': STEM Students Say They Walked Out of Event in Order to Hold Their Own Vigil," Scripps Local Media, The Denver Channel, ABC 7, https://www.thedenverchannel.com/news/local-news/its-about-kendrick-stem-students-say-they-walked-out-of-event-in-order-to-hold-their-own-vigil.

3. U.S. Const. amend. II, America's Founding Documents, The Bill of Rights: A Transcription, National Archives, https://www.archives.gov/founding-docs/bill-of-rights-transcript#toc-amendment-ii-2.

4. George Washington to Alexander Hamilton, May 2, 1783, Mount Vernon, VA, https://www.mountvernon.org/library/digitalhistory/quotes/article/it-may-be-laid-down-as-a-primary-position-and-the-basis-of-our-system-that-every-citizen-who-enjoys-the-protection-of-a-free-government-owes-not-only-a-proportion-of-his-property-but-even-his-personal-services-to-the-defence-of-it-and-consequently-that-th/.

5. Thomas Jefferson to William Stephens Smith, November 13, 1787, Library of Congress, Washington, DC, https://www.loc.gov/exhibits/jefferson/105.html.

6. John Gramlich and Katherine Schaeffer, "7 Facts About Guns in the U.S.," FactTank, Pew Research Center, October 22, 2019, https://www.pewresearch.org/fact-tank/2019/10/22/facts-about -guns-in-united-states/.

Chapter 5: On Biblical Environmentalism

1. Peter Ferrara, "The Great Depression Was Ended by the End of World War II, Not the Start of It," *Forbes*, November 30, 2013, https://www.forbes.com/sites/peterferrara/2013/11/30 /the-great-depression-was-ended-by-the-end-of-world-war-ii-not -the-start-of-it/#748a232757d3.
2. Zachary B. Wold, "Here's What the Green New Deal Actually Says," CNN, February 14, 2019, https://www.cnn.com/2019 /02/14/politics/green-new-deal-proposal-breakdown/index.html.
3. Brittany De Lea, "How Much AOC's Green New Deal Could Cost the Average American Household," Fox Business, July 30, 2019, https://www.foxbusiness.com/economy/aoc-green-new -deal-cost-american-household.
4. Ari Natter, "Alexandria Ocasio-Cortez's Green New Deal Could Cost $93 Trillion, Group Says," Bloomberg, February 25, 2019, https://www.bloomberg.com/news/articles/2019–02–25 /group-sees-ocasio-cortez-s-green-new-deal-costing-93-trillion.
5. Louis Casiano, "Ocasio-Cortez Responds After Report Accuses Her of 'Green New Deal' Hypocrisy: 'I Also Fly & Use A/C,'" Fox News, March 3, 2019, https://www.foxnews .com/politics/ocasio-cortez-responds-to-criticism-of-travel -methods-while-pushing-to-address-climate-change.
6. For a helpful diagram illustrating how the earth's tilt affects the seasons, see "Resource Library: Encyclopedia Entry: Axis," National Geographic, n.d., https://www.nationalgeographic.org /encyclopedia/axis/, accessed November 29, 2019.

Chapter 6: On Life According to the King

1. Melanie Arter, "New York Gov. Andrew Cuomo Signs Law Legalizing Late-Term Abortion," CBS News, January 23, 2019,

https://www.cnsnews.com/news/article/melanie-arter/new
-york-gov-cuomo-signs-law-bill-legalizing-late-term-abortion.

2. Andrew M. Cuomo, "Video, B-Roll, Audio, Photos & Rush
Transcript: Governor Cuomo Signs Legislation Protecting Women's
Reproductive Rights," New York State, January 22, 2019, https://
www.governor.ny.gov/news/video-b-roll-audio-photos-rush
-transcript-governor-cuomo-signs-legislation-protecting-womens.

3. "VA Gov on Abortion: 'Infant Would Be Resuscitated If That's
What the Mother and the Family Desired,'" *Vox*, February 1,
2019, https://www.vox.com/2019/2/1/18205428/virginia-abortion
-bill-kathy-tran-ralph-northam.

4. Roe v. Wade, 410 U.S. at 158 (1973).

Chapter 7: For the American Family

1. W. Bradford Wilcox, "The Evolution of Divorce," *National
Affairs*, Fall 2009, https://www.nationalaffairs.com/publications
/detail/the-evolution-of-divorce.

2. Belinda Luscombe, "The Divorce Rate Is Dropping. That May
Not Actually Be Good News," *Time*, November 26, 2018, https://
time.com/5434949/divorce-rate-children-marriage-benefits/.

3. Amy Desai shares this research in her *Focus on the Family* article,
"How Could Divorce Affect My Kids?" January 1, 2007, https://
www.focusonthefamily.com/marriage/how-could-divorce
-affect-my-kids/.

4. Bradford Wilcox, *Why Marriage Matters: Twenty-six
Conclusions from the Social Sciences*, 2nd ed. (New York:
Institute for American Values, 2005), http://americanvalues.
org/catalog/pdfs/why_marriage_matters2.pdf.

Chapter 8: For Kingdom-Centered Healthcare

1. Yoni Blumerg, "70% of Americans Now Support Medicare-
for-all—here's how single-payer could affect you," CNBC,
August 28, 2018, https://www.cnbc.com/2018/08/28/most
-americans-now-support-medicare-for-all-and-free-college
-tuition.html.

2. Abigail Abrams, "Where the 2020 Democratic Candidates Stand on Medicare For All," *Time*, July 31, 2019, https://time.com/5616864/2020-democratic-candidates-health-care/; see also Kevin Uhrmacher et al., "Where 2020 Democrats Stand on Health Care," *Washington Post*, January 23, 2020, https://www.washingtonpost.com/graphics/politics/policy-2020/medicare-for-all/.

Chapter 11: Changing America Through Kingdom Living

1. "America's Founding Documents: Declaration of Independence: A Transcription," National Archives, Washington, DC, https://www.archives.gov/founding-docs/declaration-transcript.

ABOUT THE AUTHOR

Phil Robertson is a professional hunter who invented his own duck call and founded the successful Duck Commander Company. He also starred in the popular television series on A&E, *Duck Dynasty*, and is now the cohost of the hugely popular podcast, *Unashamed with Phil & Jase Robertson*. He is the *New York Times* bestselling author of *Jesus Politics*; *The Theft of America's Soul*; *Happy, Happy, Happy*; and *UnPHILtered*. He and his wife, Kay, live in West Monroe, Louisiana. He has five children, nineteen grandchildren, and thirteen great-grandchildren.